best hikes with dogs
INLAND NORTHWEST

best hikes with dogs

INLAND NORTHWEST

**Craig Romano
& Alan L. Bauer**

THE MOUNTAINEERS BOOKS

THE MOUNTAINEERS BOOKS

is the nonprofit publishing arm of The Mountaineers, an organization founded in 1906 and dedicated to the exploration, preservation, and enjoyment of outdoor and wilderness areas.

1001 SW Klickitat Way, Suite 201, Seattle, WA 98134

© 2005 by Craig Romano and Alan L. Bauer

First edition: First printing 2005, second printing 2013

Manufactured in the United States of America

Acquiring Editor: Cassandra Conyers
Project Editor: Laura Drury
Copy Editor: Colin Chisholm
Cover and Book Design: The Mountaineers Books
Layout: Judy Petry
Cartographer: Pease Press Cartography
All photographs by Alan L. Bauer unless otherwise noted.

Cover photograph: *Mittens*
Frontispiece: *Sailor takes a break along the trail.*

Maps shown in this book were produced using National Geographic TOPO! software. For more information, go to www.nationalgeographic.com/topo.

Library of Congress Cataloging-in-Publication Data
Romano, Craig.
   Best hikes with dogs. Inland Northwest / Craig Romano and Alan L. Bauer. — 1st ed.
      p. cm.
   Includes index.
   ISBN 0-89886-858-0
   1. Hiking with dogs—Inland Empire—Guidebooks. 2. Hiking with dogs—British Columbia—Guidebooks. 3. Inland Empire—Guidebooks. 4. British Columbia—Guidebooks.   I. Bauer, Alan. II. Title.
SF427.455.R66 2004
796.51'09797—dc22

   2004023957

ISBN (paperback): 978-0-89886-858-6
ISBN (ebook): 978-1-59485-171-1

TABLE OF CONTENTS

Map Legend

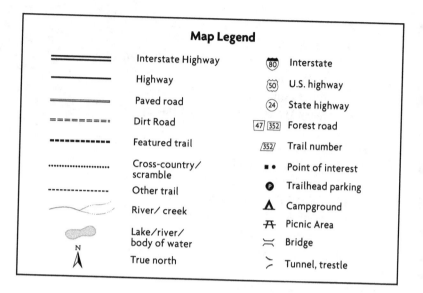

═══	Interstate Highway	🛡80	Interstate
────	Highway	🛡50	U.S. highway
═══	Paved road	24	State highway
=========	Dirt Road	47 352	Forest road
------------	Featured trail	352	Trail number
....	Cross-country/ scramble	▪•	Point of interest
----------	Other trail	Ⓟ	Trailhead parking
∿	River/ creek	▲	Campground
⬭	Lake/river/ body of water	☶	Picnic Area
N ⬆	True north	⤫	Bridge
		⤳	Tunnel, trestle

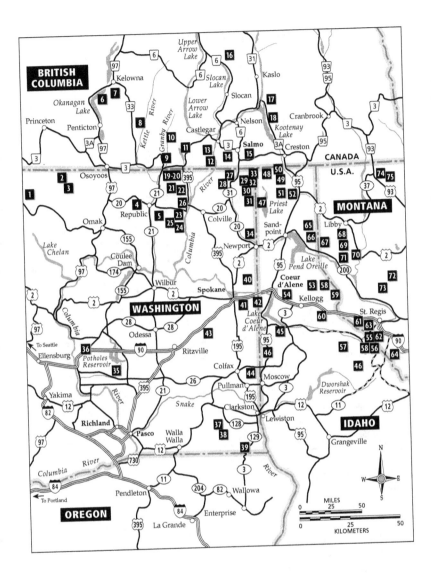

HIKE SUMMARY TABLE

Hike	Easy on Paws	Easy Hike 4 miles or less	Possible overnight trip	Alongside streams most of the hike	Lake(s) to swim in	Unleashed okay	Solitude	Alpine scenery	Forested trail for the entire hike	Good for senior dogs	Best for well-conditioned dogs
1. Tiffany Mountain and Lake			•		•	•		•			•
2. Snowshoe Meadow	•		•	•		•	•		•		•
3. Disappointment Peak						•	•	•			
4. Fir Mountain	•					•	•	•	•		
5. Swan Lake and Butte	•	•			•				•	•	
6. Wildhorse Canyon			•						•		•
7. Myra Canyon	•									•	
8. Collier Lakes	•	•	•		•	•				•	•
9. Thimble Mountain						•		•			
10. Granby River			•	•		•	•		•		
11. Deer Point-Christina Lake	•		•	•						•	
12. Record Ridge						•		•			•
13. Old Glory						•		•			•
14. Champion Lakes	•	•			•				•	•	
15. Panther Lake			•	•		•	•		•	•	
16. Wilson Creek			•	•		•			•		
17. Pilot Bay	•	•			•				•	•	
18. Lockhart Creek	•		•	•		•	•			•	
19. Big Lick	•		•	•		•	•		•	•	
20. Mount Leona	•					•	•	•	•		
21. Copper Butte	•					•	•	•			
22. Wapaloosie Mountain	•					•		•			•
23. Snow Peak Cabin			•			•		•			
24. Barnaby Buttes	•					•	•	•	•		
25. Kettle Crest South			•			•	•	•			•

Hike	Easy on Paws	Easy Hike 4 miles or less	Possible overnight trip	Alongside streams most of the hike	Lake(s) to swim in	Unleashed okay	Solitude	Alpine scenery	Forested trail for the entire hike	Good for senior dogs	Best for well-conditioned dogs
26. Emerald Lake	•		•	•	•				•	•	
27. Abercrombie Mountain						•		•			•
28. South Fork Silver Creek	•		•			•	•		•		
29. Sullivan Lake	•			•					•	•	
30. Noisy Creek–Hall Mountain	•			•		•		•			•
31. Grassy Top Mountain	•					•		•		•	
32. Thunder Mountain Loop			•			•	•	•	•		•
33. Salmo Loop–Little Snowy Top			•			•	•	•			•
34. Bead Lake	•		•	•	•				•	•	
35. Blythe and Chukar Lakes			•							•	
36. Dusty Lake		•		•						•	
37. Tucannon River	•		•	•		•			•	•	
38. Oregon Butte Grand Loop			•			•			•		•
39. Puffer Butte	•	•						•	•	•	
40. Day Mountain Loop-Mount Spokane State Park	•								•	•	
41. Iller Creek Conservation Area	•	•								•	
42. Liberty Lake Loop	•			•	•				•	•	
43. Cheever Lake Headquarters Trail			•		•					•	
44. Kamiak Butte	•	•						•		•	
45. Indian Cliff	•	•			•			•		•	
46. Mary Minerva McCroskey Country	•	•					•	•	•	•	
47. Priest Lake-Lakeshore Trail	•			•	•					•	•
48. Upper Priest River	•			•	•		•	•		•	•
49. Pyramid and Ball Lakes	•	•	•		•	•			•	•	•
50. West Fork Lake and Mountain			•		•	•	•	•	•		•

Hike	Easy on Paws	Easy Hike 4 miles or less	Possible overnight trip	Alongside streams most of the hike	Lake(s) to swim in	Unleashed okay	Solitude	Alpine scenery	Forested trail for the entire hike	Good for senior dogs	Best for well-conditioned dogs
51. Snow Lake			•	•	•	•	•				
52. Deep Creek-Kootenai National Wildlife Refuge	•	•	•							•	
53. Upper Coeur d'Alene River	•		•	•		•				•	
54. Marie Creek	•		•	•	•	•			•	•	
55. Simmons Creek				•	•	•	•				
56. Upper St. Joe River			•	•		•			•	•	
57. Mallard Lake and Peak			•		•	•	•	•	•	•	
58. Settlers Grove Cedars-West Fork Eagle Creek				•						•	•
59. Revett Lake	•	•	•		•	•		•			•
60. Lone Lake					•	•	•	•	•		
61. Crystal Lake		•	•		•	•	•		•		
62. Hazel and Hub Lakes			•	•	•	•	•	•			
63. Diamond and Cliff Lakes	•	•	•		•					•	•
64. Heart and Pearl Lakes			•		•	•		•			
65. Calder Mountain-Pend Oreille Divide					•	•	•				•
66. Moose Lake and Mountain	•		•		•	•		•	•		•
67. Little Spar Lake			•	•	•	•		•			
68. Little Ibex Lake			•	•	•	•	•	•			•
69. Saint Paul Lake	•		•	•	•	•			•	•	
70. Bramlet Lake		•	•		•	•			•	•	
71. Upper Geiger Lake-Lost Buck Pass			•		•	•		•	•		
72. Cabin Lake			•		•	•		•	•	•	
73. Deer Lake			•		•	•	•	•			•
74. Bluebird Lake-Highline			•		•	•		•		•	
75. Stahl Peak Lookout					•	•	•	•	•	•	•

ACKNOWLEDGMENTS

Author's Note

Researching and writing this book have been an adventure, a pleasure, and a lot of hard work. But always a labor of love. However, even with all of my own dogged determination I couldn't have possibly put this book together without the help and cooperation of so many others. First and foremost, a big thank-you goes out to my book partners, Alan Bauer and Mittens. Without you two I'd be barking up the wrong tree! A big thanks, too, to Cassandra Conyers for helping me bring this project to fruition. I'd also like to thank all the dogs out there for adding their input and paw prints to these hikes. Jax, Gherry, Barkley, Autumn, Sasha, Buddy, Lida, Ollie—you guys are top dogs! A big lick of gratitude also goes out to Lynn Olafson for providing great company in the Selkirks, and to Jerry Grazer for providing great accommodations in the Kettles. Thanks, too, to all the land managers who provided their time to help in my research. Wayne Kopischke of the Priest Lake Ranger District and Dan Reibin of the Castlegar BC Forest District were especially helpful. A special thanks to Doug Romano for accompanying me in the wildlands of Montana. And, of course, the biggest thanks goes to my number-one hiking companion and love of my life, Heather Scott. All of you deserve a great big Scooby Snack for all of your help and guidance!

Photographer's Note

The grandeur of the lands covered within this project made photography a pure joy over the past two summers. It also had intense challenges: severe heat in 2003, smoke from fires, and dodging bears and thunderstorms, all while trying to capture the beauty seen through the eyes of our dog friends. I'd like to thank The Mountaineers Books for teaming up Craig and me for this adventure—we have surely become life friends. What can I say about my main sidekick, Mittens, who traveled over 8,000 miles in the rig with me over some of the roughest roads imaginable. She never argued with me; she never told me to slow down; and she pointed out more elk and grouse than I had seen in a lifetime prior. Lastly, I wish to give the utmost thanks to my family—Lois, Elizabeth, and Christopher. Without your understanding in allowing Mittens and me to venture away 3–5 days at a time, I could have never witnessed these lands, step by step.

Mittens and her human, the photographer, hike the trail atop Puffer Butte.

Mittens' Note

Hey, I'm the only native to these landscapes, so it was a good thing I was a part of this project! I was born in Pullman, Washington, so this stuff is second nature to me. I want to give a booming "Woof!" to the Bauer family for rescuing me from the Whitman County Humane Society in Pullman. If they hadn't traveled all the way across Washington State to pick me up I would have never been blessed with such a loving family. And hey, now I've gotten to sleep in motels across three states and in Canada. I also would like to thank Dr. Teri Weronko at the Snoqualmie Valley Animal Hospital in Fall City. She helps keep me smiling and healthy—and she signed the papers so that I could go to Canada and back!

PREFACE

I've never known a dog to toss a beer can on the trail, leave a campfire unattended, or carve his name into a tree. Inconsiderate acts all done by thoughtless hikers. Yet despite the fact that some hikers are not good stewards of the land, we don't call for an outright ban on people on the trails. Many hikers, however, would be content barring man's best friend from the trails. Perhaps they have had negative encounters with mean dogs (or worse, mean owners). Perhaps they have witnessed dogs terrorizing wildlife. Perhaps they vividly (and olfactorily) remember stepping in doggie-doo en route to their favorite alpine lake. And because of these negative experiences, they believe that dogs have no place in the wilderness. Responsible dog owners believe differently. We acknowledge that dogs do have some impact, but that this impact may be marginal compared to other human impacts. For example, a well-trained and well-behaved dog probably does less damage to a trail than, say, a 200-pound backpacker. We also suspect that our dog's keen senses may increase rather than decrease our awareness of wildlife. Most importantly, we know that our backcountry experiences with our furry buddies are precious. They never complain when it rains; they listen to us while we curse during steep ascents; they offer us protection and company; and they always put smiles on our faces at the end of long days. Dogs make great hiking companions, but like we humans they must be well-trained and well-behaved before taking to the trails. That's where responsible owners come in. We have an obligation not only to make sure that both ourselves and our dogs respect the wilderness, but also to act as ambassadors, assuring fellow trail users that canines belong on the trails as much as any biped. We may not convince everyone of that, but by being good pet owners and good stewards, we'll help keep our trails open to our dogs. Heck, who knows, we might even be able to train some of our dogs to help clean up after thoughtless hikers!

Next page: Western hemlocks near Panther Lake

PART 1

Hiking with Your Dog

Biscuit shows off her bells.

Good Dogs Require Good Owners

Just as you had to learn backcountry basics before hitting the trails, so will your dog. Only this time you are the teacher. It's important not only that you properly condition and train your dog to be a good hiker, but also that your dog be a good trail user. What does that mean? First—this may seem obvious—your dog should be friendly! Not only to you, but also to other hikers and dogs. Unfriendly or aggressive dogs shouldn't be on the trail.

Your dog should be fit. Just like you. Dragging your plump pup up a steep trail may be seen as animal cruelty to passersby. Besides, it's not fair to your poor buddy. Even if your pooch is in top-notch shape, there are trails that aren't right for him—perhaps too steep, too dry, too much exposure, too difficult, or maybe just too busy. Some trails prohibit dogs. Please respect that. Nothing will rile up the anti-dog contingency more than seeing a dog on a restricted trail. Respect leash laws as well. I have made an effort in this book to describe trails where your dog can hike unrestrained, but a few of my selected hikes require leashes. Don't give the anti-dog people a reason to ban our dogs from these trails.

Your dog should also be amicable to wildlife. If Rover loves to chase squirrels or harass geese, obedience school is in order. If you condone his grouse growling, then perhaps a little obedience school is in order for you! A good dog will help you observe wildlife, not repel it.

One of the biggest complaints you'll hear about dogs on the trails involves their excrement. Every effort should be made to properly dispose of these doggie treats. Pack it out or bury it, always at least 200 feet from any trail, campsite, or water source. Dogs, too, must practice Leave No Trace ethics. Again, that's where we get to be the teachers. Let's hope our students hound us for information.

Doggie Fitness

Although our domestic buddies have inherited instincts from their wilder cousins—that doesn't necessarily mean that they're ready to spring into action in the backcountry. Domestic life has a way of making you soft—just look at many a dog's owner for proof. And just as we need to condition ourselves by building up strength and fitness before hitting the trail, so does your dog.

Before bringing Spot on his first hike, it's a good idea to start a walking regimen. Start slowly and work up in both distance and intensity. Allow your puppy some time to develop. Pushing a dog too early can be detrimental to his physical development. It's important, too, that you allow time for your dog's sensitive foot pads to toughen up. They won't callous like ours, but over time they'll be able to handle the uneven and sometimes rocky terrain of a trail. One of the best conditioning exercises for hiking is running. Running conditions the body to better absorb impact, builds muscle mass, and strengthens joints. However, running can also cause overuse injuries. Dogs develop the same types of running injuries that humans do, such as tendonitis, torn ligaments, and muscle soreness. Don't overdo it. Build up slowly and listen to your body—and to your dog.

Like humans, dogs come in all sizes and shapes. We all respond to exercise and impact differently. Pugs and Pomeranians are capable of being trail dogs, too. But their physical limitations will determine how far and fast they can go, as well as the type of terrain they can handle. You may be a greyhound but your dachshund isn't.

A regular running or walking regimen with your dog is also a great way to condition her for new terrain, people, other dogs, and unusual situations—all while building up a camaraderie with you. Be sure that your dog eats properly (but not right before exercising) and takes in plenty of water while out walking, running, or hiking. It's not a bad idea to have your dog checked by a veterinarian before beginning an exercise program.

Your vet may find a preexisting condition that may warrant special care or attention. In time, the two of you will be in good shape and ready to hit the trail.

And what about tired old dogs? They need exercise, too. There are still trails suited for them, but you will need to be extra patient while hiking with ol' Yeller. The joy of just being out with your best friend will more than compensate for any lack of distance covered.

Permits and Regulations

Okay now, the two of you have been jogging around the block all spring and you're ready to hit the trail. Where to hike? The Inland Northwest is blessed with millions of acres of public lands and thousands of miles of trails. But can you bring your dog on all of those trails? For the most part, yes. Very few agencies restrict dogs from taking to the trails. The National Park Service is one of them—and whether you agree or not with their dog bans, the percentage of land they manage in the Inland Northwest is quite small. Some provincial parks such as Kokanee Glacier and Valhalla do not allow dogs. Reasons for banning dogs often center around wildlife management—in the case of these two parks, high concentrations of grizzly bears. Some places may prohibit dogs simply to provide other trail users with a dog-free environment. I love dogs, but I also understand the need to keep them out of certain places. Please obey the rules and regulations that govern an area. Acts of doggie civil-disobedience (a pant-in?) may land you with not only a fine, but also malice from fellow trail users. This works against our cause. Besides, your dog doesn't need this headache—he just wants to go hiking.

As far as permits and regulations for humans, there are very few in the Inland Northwest—unlike the coastal areas of the Pacific Northwest where it seems that a pass or permit is needed for just about everywhere. In this book the Northwest Trail Pass is needed only for the Umatilla National Forest (Blue Mountains), and for the Kettle Crest Trail in the Colville National Forest if you park at Sherman Pass. There are no other passes needed for hikes on national forest lands in this book. Hikes on national wildlife refuges mentioned in this guide require a permit. State parks, too, in both Washington and Idaho. Day-use passes can be purchased in the individual parks (typically $5 per car for Washington and $3 per car in Idaho). Consider purchasing annual passes if you plan on

Opposite: Heather and Lynn (humans) with Autumn and Barkley at Saint Paul Lake (Photo by Craig Romano)

Sailor and her human, Sydney Mullock

making many visits ($50 in Washington, $25 in Idaho). Several hikes in this volume involve lands managed by the U.S. Fish and Wildlife Service. These national wildlife refuges require a day-use fee (typically $3 per car). They can be purchased at the refuge. A Golden Eagle Pass upgraded with a U.S. National Wildlife Refuge sticker ($65) allows you unlimited visits to all refuges for a year.

Most of the car campgrounds mentioned in this guide also require a fee. Except for those managed by the British Columbia Forest Service, these fees can be paid directly at the campgrounds.

Canada

What about Canada, eh? Do I need any special documentation to bring my dog north of the border? Yes, but it's not too complicated. Your dog must be able to provide a certificate signed by a licensed veterinarian that clearly describes him and declares that he has been vaccinated against rabies within the past twelve or thirty-six months, depending upon the type of vaccine. Dogs under three months old don't need this certification, but then you have to prove his age. Furthermore, three-month-old pups shouldn't be on the trail yet!

You'll also need this documentation to bring your buddy back home with you. (**Note:** A collar tag is not considered sufficient proof of immunization.) As far as you, well, you need some documentation, too. Proof of citizenship must be carried. A certified birth certificate and photo ID is usually sufficient. Although not required, I always bring my passport. Border crossings aren't as smooth as they used to be. A passport is the best proof of citizenship.

Also be aware that certain food items are not allowed to cross the border. Meat and dairy are prohibited, and this may go for certain dog foods, too. You may want to purchase your doggie treats in Canada. The labels will give your French poodle something to read.

Go Lightly on the Land

I'll never forget my encounter with Charlie. I met this mixed-breed hiking pooch on the very popular Maple Pass Trail off the North Cascades Highway. Donning his own pack and decked out in a styling Southwestern-motif bandana, Charlie sauntered down the busy trail, his party in tow. Mild-mannered and mindful of his environment, Charlie practiced what we preach—go lightly on the land. Although there were snow patches on the trail, Charlie never stepped off it. Nor did he gallop across the meadows when muddy sections replaced solid tread in the well-trodden trail. Even more remarkable, Charlie didn't have to be told to stay on the trail. He knew!

After meeting this environmentally friendly trail user, I continued on to the heather meadows of Maple Pass. There I witnessed a good number of biped visitors running all over the place. Unfortunately, "the place" didn't seem to include the trail. It meant stomping meadows and crushing flowers. "Where's Charlie now?" I sighed. "We really can use

Barkley and Sasha resting along the trail (Photo by Craig Romano)

his guidance and good example." And if Charlie could speak in a way that we humans could understand, I'm sure he would bark out the following Leave No Trace principles about going lightly on the land:

Travel and camp on durable surfaces

Dog and hiker should stay on the trail if one exists. When traveling cross-country make every effort to stick to hard surfaces and snow. If your group must cross a meadow, fan out in order to distribute impact. When camping, use existing sites whenever possible. Otherwise camp on hard surfaces. If you must camp in grassy areas, minimize the time your tent covers vegetation. Don't wear new trails to your water sources. Utilize a water bladder to minimize trips to lakes, creeks, or springs. Don't cut switchbacks—this includes your dog, who just can't wait to get there!

Dispose of wastes properly

Always use a privy if available. For your dog that may be problematic, but if you dispose of his fecal waste in a privy make sure the plastic bag doesn't go in with it. When no privy exists, do your business (this goes for the both of you) at least 200 feet from any trail, water source, or campsite. And—this may sound sacrilegious to your dog—dig a "cat hole" and bury all feces.

Leave what you find

You know the old adage, "Leave only footsteps. Take only pictures." Please leave plants, animals, and historic artifacts alone. Trail signs aren't souvenirs. Don't pick flowers. Your dog must resist chewing on those flowers—he doesn't know the difference between a common and endangered variety. (I wish he knew a good way of getting rid of Scotch broom and Eurasian milfoil though!) And although it's okay for ground squirrels and grizzlies to dig in the backcountry, it's not okay for Rover. Keep his excavations confined to your backyard.

Minimize campfire impacts

The use of a backcountry stove is highly recommended. Be extra careful in tinder-dry areas. Clear needles and bark (not your dog's) away from your stove's base. Never make a campfire in an alpine zone where wood is a precious commodity. If you must make a fire, use extreme caution. Only use dead and downed wood. Don't expect your dog to collect it for you.

Upper Geiger Lake seen from Lost Buck Pass (Photo by Craig Romano)

Respect wildlife

Never get too close to wild animals. They may be frightened, and mothers may be forced to abandon their litters, broods, etc. Your dog should not bark at, chase, or in any way harass wildlife. Irresponsible dog owners allowing their pets to do so have caused many people to oppose allowing dogs on trails.

Hiking with a dog can greatly increase your wildlife observations, because your dog has keen olfactory and auditory senses. Let him help you enjoy your surroundings, but the both of you should always be respectful of those surroundings and the critters that call it home.

Water

Dogs love to swim, splash, and soak. Many of the hikes in this guide lead to lakes and creeks where it's assumed your pup will go for a splash. Heck, perhaps you will, too—it gets pretty hot in the Inland Northwest during July and August. But make sure that your dog doesn't plop his sweaty little body in a spring or pool that is used as a potable water supply. Good judgment here is required on your part.

Plan ahead and prepare

Know your route and know what type of conditions will be encountered before stepping out the door. Be sure that you and your pup are properly prepared for changing conditions. Carry extra food, water, clothing, and shelter. This will not only protect you in case of an emergency, but also protect the environment from you having to scavenge food and materials.

Good Canine Trail Etiquette

All trail users need to practice good trail etiquette, which includes respecting the environment and displaying courtesy to fellow trail users. A smile can go a long way, but we need to do more than just be nice when we're out hiking. We need to be conscious of others around us and allow them the very things we expect in return: tranquility and respect. By being model trail users you and your dog will set an example, making it easier for other users to accept your pooch's presence out in nature. Please be good trail ambassadors.

Your dog should always be with you while on the trail, either on a leash or under strict voice control. Although the majority of hikes in this book are on trails where leashes are not required, there are many

Sailor leads the way along Fir Mountain Trail.

cases where it's still the prudent (and courteous) thing to do. When should your dog be leashed? For a start, whenever there are many other trail users. You may have the world's most lovable dog, but some people just don't like dogs. They may even be afraid of them, or allergic to them. And most people, including this author, are always a little alarmed when they see a strange dog charging down the trail towards them. To a small child this can be traumatizing.

Dogs should also be on leashes in areas where there is a lot of wild-life, especially bears. In rattlesnake country, too, a leash will do your dog good (perhaps even save his life). Spring and early summer, when wild critters are rearing their young, are good times to keep old Scratch leashed.

Leashed or not, your dog should also know the following commands: "Come," "Wait," and "Leave it." The first two are essential to minimize conflicts with other trail users. They also keep your dog safe so that you may assess a situation. The last command is primarily for your dog's safety. The last thing you want your buddy to do is to try out some new trail snack. In the first-aid section of this book I go into further detail on what you don't want your buddy sampling.

Be considerate of other visitors

You and your dog share the trails with many other users. The following section explains proper procedures when encountering other hikers, cyclists, and equestrians. Never leave an area unsightly. Always pack out what you pack in. Food scraps are litter and may attract wildlife such as bears. If your dog "drops one" on the trail, clean it up.

Check out *www.lnt.org* for more information.

Dealing with other trail users

Hikers. Yield to other hikers. Step clear of the trail to allow them to pass. Many people will want to stop and meet a well-behaved dog, but others just want to pass by without being sniffed.

Horses. Once again the two of you need to yield and step clear off the trail. If possible step down from the trail so that you are lower than the horse. Horses are easily spooked. It is absolutely imperative that you keep your dog quiet and calm.

Cyclists. You and Fido should once again yield the right-of-way. It is far easier for you and your dog to step to the side of the trail than it is for a cyclist to dismount and move around you. Most cyclists will slow down and let you know of their passing. Good control of your dog will ensure your dog's and the cyclist's safety.

Motorcyclists. All but one or two hikes in this book are closed to motorized users. But in case you do encounter one, motorcyclists are supposed to yield to hikers. Since you have your dog with you though, the two of you should step to the side of the trail and let them pass.

With your buddy under control, safe passage is guaranteed for all.

Gear for Fido and You

Proper gear can make all the difference between having a wonderful time or a nightmare experience. There's no one size fits all when it comes to picking out gear. Different folks like different strokes. You need to find out for yourself what works best for you.

First and foremost is good footwear. What type of shoe you decide to go with (low top, leather, etc.) will depend on your frame, strength, comfort, and the type of terrain you'll be traveling over. But be sure that your shoes fit properly and offer support.

As far as your dog goes, footwear is not a bad thing to consider

Biscuit breaks in a new pack.

either. Every effort has been made in this book to take Rover on trails that won't cause serious discomfort to his foot pads. But rocky sections and snow are sometimes unavoidable. Consider carrying dog booties for these situations. Look for booties that offer good traction, and, as with your own boots, make sure that your dog's booties are not too tight or loose. Remember, too, that your dog sweats through his feet, so allow him to cool off from time to time if he is donning booties on a warm day.

Having a good pack is important, and, as with boots, the pack you choose will depend on your personal preferences. Your dog should wear a pack, too, so that he can carry his essentials (listed further down). The pack should fit snugly and the weight should be equally distributed. Most dogs are capable of carrying 20 percent of their weight. If the two of you are going out for the night, you may want to consider bringing some type of sleeping pad for your buddy. If it's cold, an insulating device might not be a bad idea either—otherwise prepare to share your sleeping bag with him (and you thought your spouse's morning breath was bad!).

There are some good books out that deal specifically with gear and equipment for hiking and backpacking. Please refer to the Recommended Reading section in Appendix A.

The 10 Essentials for Humans

1. **Map and compass.** This is especially important if you plan on exploring off-trail. Be sure you know how to use them.
2. **Sun protection.** Even in the wet Cascades I always carry sunscreen and sunglasses. At higher elevations your exposure to UV rays is much more intense than at sea level. Snow and water may intensify burning. Protect yourself.
3. **Extra clothing.** It may be 70°F at the trailhead, but at the summit it's 45 and windy. Storms can and do blow in rapidly. In the high country it can snow any time of the year. Be sure to carry raingear, wind gear, and extra layers.
4. **Headlamp or flashlight.** An injury or poor planning may force you to spend the night. Be prepared to hike out in the dark.
5. **First-aid supplies.** At the very least your kit should include bandages, gauze, scissors, tape, tweezers, pain relievers, antiseptics, and perhaps a small manual. It is also recommended that you receive first-aid training through a program such as MOFA (Mountaineering and Outdoor First Aid).
6. **Firestarter (matches or a lighter).** Be sure you keep your matches dry. I use ziplock bags. A candle can come in handy, too.
7. **Knife.** The ubiquitous Swiss Army knife is a must. Multi-tools also work well but may be heavier.
8. **Extra food.** Always pack in more food than what you think you need. I also always pack a couple of energy sports bars for emergencies.
9. **Extra water.** I carry two full water bottles all the time, unless I'm hiking entirely along a water source. You'll need to carry iodine tablets or a filter to avoid catching any waterborne nasties such as *giardia*.
10. **Emergency shelter.** A space blanket or poncho can easily be transformed into an emergency tent. Consider packing some rope, too.

Most hikers don't leave home without other tried, true, and trusted items. Just about everyone out there has an opinion on what their "eleventh" essential is. This topic makes for some good discussions. Ask others what they bring. For me the eleventh essential is duct tape. This stuff can perform miracles, from mending wounds and equipment to creating utensils and hats.

The 10 Essentials for Canines

1. **Obedience training.** Your dog must be able to behave properly around other dogs, people, and wildlife.
2. **Doggie backpack.** Your dog should be able to carry his own gear. Otherwise you are looking at a heavier load. Unless you double as a Sherpa, let your shar-pei carry her own.
3. **First-aid kit.** Details listed further down.
4. **Dog food and treats.** As with your own supply, carry more dog food than you think your pooch will need. Also consider that your dog will be burning more calories than when the two of you sit at home and watch *Best in Show*. Scooby Snacks are a good idea as well.
5. **Water and bowl.** Your dog has to intake sufficient fluids, too. A lightweight collapsible bowl will make it easier for her to drink.
6. **Leash and harness or collar.** Always carry one even if it is not

Dan Nelson and Parka hike during hunting season.

required on the trail. A situation may arise that warrants lassoing your Lassie.

7. **Insect repellent.** Mosquitoes love dog blood, too. But before dousing your dog with DEET, be sure that he doesn't have any negative reactions to it. And use it sparingly. Be sure that he can't lick where you apply it. Ticks are also a concern on some trails and can be thwarted by applying Frontline. This topical application will work for up to one month, repelling both ticks and fleas.

8. **ID tags and picture identification.** Like hikers, dogs can get lost. Be sure your dog has his ID tags on. Carrying a picture can help others identify your dog. For all George Orwell fans, consider having your dog microchipped.

9. **Dog booties.** Good for protecting your dog's feet on rough terrain, good for traction on snow, and good for keeping bandages in place if your buddy injures his paw.

10. **Plastic bags and trowel.** You'll need the bags to collect any presents your dog may leave on the trail. If you're on a popular trail, pack it out. Otherwise use your trowel to dig a small hole (away from water sources) and bury it.

As far as an eleventh essential for Fido? A brush certainly comes in handy, especially if your buddy is of the long-hair persuasion. A brush will help remove seeds and other debris and may also reveal tenacious ticks.

Canine First Aid

Hiking dogs face many of the same perils that we do. Like humans, dogs should only hike on trails and terrain within their abilities. They should be properly conditioned for what they are about to embark on (yes, pun intended). And like us, our dogs need to be prepared for the unexpected. Many of our first-aid items can be used on our four-legged companions. But we should also have a first-aid kit for Fido. In it should be the following items (if not already in your kit):

- Gauze pads and roll
- Adhesive tape
- Tweezers
- Scissors
- Toenail clippers
- Rectal thermometer (**Note:** A healthy dog's temperature should read 101°F)

- Hydrogen peroxide
- Betadine
- Canine eye wash
- Calamine lotion
- Antibiotic ointments
- Baking soda
  (for bee stings)
- Petroleum jelly
- Buffered aspirin
- Antacid

Be aware that certain medications, foods, and substances that we humans ingest can make your dog seriously ill, or worse, kill him. Acetaminophen (Tylenol), even in small dosages, can kill a dog. Ibuprofen (Advil) may also be harmful. Check with your vet before giving your pooch any type of medication. Coated aspirin (one tablet only) is generally considered

Sailor drinks water from her human's bottle.

safe for dogs, but check with your veterinarian for the right dosage.

Don't give your chocolate Lab (or any other dog) chocolate. It can kill him, especially baking chocolate. (If I were a dog I'd be a goner!) And make sure that your dog stays away from salmon and trout. A small amount of ingested raw or dead salmon can kill your dog. (It's actually not the fish but a parasite that these fish carry.) Be vigilant around lakes that may host anglers. Most of these outdoorsy people are pretty good at cleaning up, but occasionally fish guts are left behind. It's a good idea to keep your dog away from the water when dead salmon are washing up along the shore (as during spawning). If your dog does eat salmon, trout, or any other potentially toxic substance, immediately induce vomiting. This can be done by administering hydrogen peroxide. Use approximately 3 tablespoons for a 70-pound dog.

The following are other potential problems that you should be familiar with. (**Note:** This section is meant to supplement, not replace, the use of a good canine first-aid manual. It is highly recommended that you consult one.)

Heatstroke

Avoiding heat is your best defense against heatstroke. Hike during the early or later parts of the day. If the trail isn't shaded, save it for a cooler time of the year. Keep your dog hydrated at all times—before, during, and after the hike. Dogs are not equipped with the best cooling systems. They sweat only through their feet and tongues. Add a coat of black fur and it's really easy for a dog to overheat. Even on days that you may consider comfortable, it may be too hot for your best friend.

How do you know when your pooch is overheating? Early symptoms include an elevated heart rate, rapid panting, and excess saliva. Your dog's gums may turn a bright red. It is absolutely necessary that you cool her down if these symptoms are present. Get her water or get her to water.

Mittens watches a herd of elk pass on Puffer Butte.

Wet her belly. Let her rest in a shaded area. Her internal temperature should be around 101°F.

Pad Injury

Sharp rocks along the trail can puncture your buddy's paws, and hot surfaces can burn them. Be especially careful around old lookouts and mining sites, where old nails or pieces of glass may puncture or slice paws.

To treat a cut or laceration: First remove any object that may still be lodged in your dog's pads. Stop the bleeding through direct pressure, and then apply an antiseptic ointment. Finally, bandage the injured area. A bootie can be used to keep the bandage in place.

Torn dewclaws

Dewclaws, the fifth "finger" on your dog's front legs, are susceptible to catching on sharp objects. This in turn can tear it, causing excessive bleeding. Although usually not serious, a torn dewclaw will give your dog considerable discomfort. Stop the bleeding either by pressure or with styptic powder, clean the wound, and then bandage it. Use a bootie to keep the bandage in place.

Lodged Seeds

Grass seeds and foxtails can sometimes be a minor nuisance to us when they lodge into our socks and boots. When they lodge in our dogs it is a serious concern. If your dog paws excessively at his mouth, gags, or drools, he may have a seed lodged in it. Open his mouth and try to remove it with your fingers. If you can't locate it, feeding your dog bread may dislodge it. A cough suppressant administered to your buddy may help.

If your buddy is sneezing frequently, he may have a seed lodged in his nose. Once again try to remove it with your fingers. If it is too far up his nose, it'll require a trip to the vet.

Grass seeds will also occasionally find their way into your dog's ears and eyes. Use your fingers or tweezers to remove them. Flushing the eye with water will also help remove the culprits. Be sure to check your dog's feet, too. A good brushing after hiking can remove seeds that have found their way into your dog's fur.

Waterborne Critters

As a general rule you should treat all backcountry water sources. There is quite a bit of debate on how widespread nasties such as *giardia* (a

Buddy enjoys the water. (Photo by Craig Romano)

waterborne parasite) are in our water sources. New evidence suggests that the threat is greatly overblown. However, it's still better to assume that all water is contaminated. You don't want to risk it. I have contracted *giardia* on several occasions (Paraguay and Vermont) and it's no treat, especially for the people around you. Your dog, too, can contract it. Although it may be difficult to keep him from consuming untreated water, try to monitor his intake and provide treated water when possible. Keep your dog away from water seepage from mines and from sources that have been trampled by livestock. Consider seeing your vet about getting your pooch a *giardia* vaccine.

Bears

An acquaintance of mine once relayed to me a story about how his dog saved his life while hiking on the Appalachian Trail. My friend had paused at a creek to get some water. Directly across the pool he spotted a cute little bear cub, and he knew instantly that he was in danger. Momma bear was right behind him. Luckily, so was his dog. His little buddy barked, perhaps saving my friend from a mauling. Good boy!

However, there are well-documented accounts of unleashed dogs encountering bears and retreating to their owners, bringing the formidable pursuers with them. Not good.

Most of the hikes in this book are within bear country. A few lead to places where grizzlies still roam, although not in great numbers. Seeing a bear in the wild is always an awesome sight, but to minimize dangerous encounters you need to be "bear-aware":

1. When in bear country, keep your dog on a leash.
2. Make noise while you're hiking. Sing, explain your theories on life to your dog, etc.
3. Hike during daylight hours, especially in grizzly country.
4. Stay away from fresh carcasses—this is bear food.
5. Know how to identify bear sign. Fresh tracks, scat, tree scratches, overturned clumps of meadow are indications to go on high bear alert.
6. In grizzly country be vigilant along alder and willow thickets and in avalanche chutes.
7. If camping, it is imperative to keep a clean camp.
8. Avoid fish and other aromatic foods that may attract Yogi and his friends.
9. Do not leave dog bowls lying around your campsite.
10. Camp away from where you cook.
11. Hang your food away from your tent.
12. Never ever bring food into your tent.

For hikes in grizzly country it is always a good idea to call the land agency before setting out to ask if there has been any recent grizzly activity along the trail. Land agencies occasionally close trails if a sow and cub are in the area. Find a new hike if this is the case. And what do you do if the two of you do encounter a bear on the trail?

1. Always give the bear plenty of space. If he is ahead of you, wait. Be sure the trail is clear before proceeding.
2. Remain calm. Keep your dog calm, too.
3. Talk in a low voice and don't stare directly at the bear.
4. If a bear charges, don't run. The bruin may be bluffing, and the fastest hiker can't outrun the slowest bear.
5. If his charge means business, play dead. If he attacks, fight back. Your dog will probably help.

Bear attacks are rare, especially grizzly attacks. Use common sense. Respect all wildlife, especially during the rut and breeding season.

Cougars

Another wild critter that deserves the utmost respect from the both of you is the cougar. Your dog will also have to accept that this is one cat not to mess with. Although these kings of the forest instill a sense of uneasiness in many a hiker, they are quite elusive. I've seen grizzlies in the wild, but never a cougar. I have had cougars track me before, but they have never allowed me to see them. Once, on Copper Butte in the Kettle Mountains, I felt like I was being followed. Sure enough, on my way out I saw that my boot tracks were overlayed with cat tracks! So what should you do to make sure that these cats don't get fresh with you and your dog?

1. As with hiking in bear country, make lots of noise.
2. Keep your dog on a leash. The two of you close together makes you unlikely prey.
3. If you spot a cougar, don't run. Try to calm yourself and your dog.
4. Show the cougar that you're not prey. Make yourself look bigger. Wave your arms.
5. If your buddy is a little guy, pick him up and keep him close.
6. Keep eye contact with the cougar and slowly back away.
7. If the cougar attacks, throw rocks or whack the cat across the nose with a stick or a trekking pole. (I can say this in a book for dogs!) Don't bend down or turn your back on a cougar.

The chance of being attacked by a cougar is slim. However, the chance of running into a Washington State University Cougar is really good in the Inland Northwest.

Weather

By far the greatest weather concern in the mountains of the Inland Northwest is thunderstorms. You can almost always expect isolated thunderstorms during periods of hot weather, but thunderstorms move in with fronts and changing systems as well. Know the telltale signs. Cumulus clouds are usually harbingers of an incoming boomer. Stay off peaks, open ridges, and shorelines.

If you do get caught in a thunderstorm, heed the following advice:

1. Get down off summits and open ridges.
2. Seek shelter.

Summer lightning

3. Take cover in clumps of trees, but avoid tall ones or isolated groves.
4. Remove metal objects, such as trekking poles, from your pack.
5. Crouch low to the ground on the tips of your feet (to minimize contact with the ground). Cover your ears with your hands.
6. Don't whimper more than your dog.

Other Concerns

There are a few other things that you may or may not be confronted with when on a hike with your four-footed pal, but it's good to be aware of them.

Poisonous plants

Keep your dog away from poison oak and poison ivy. These plants can cause the same types of reactions that they do in humans. It is especially important that you do not let Rover chow down on these toxic plants. The presence of these plants in places like the Columbia Basin and the Kootenai River valley is a good reason to stay on trails.

Porcupines

If there are porcupines in the area, you don't want to find out about them from your dog. Keep your dog leashed, and, if camping, make sure Rover stays in the tent with you. If he gets a face full of quills it'll be a painful process for both of you to remove them. You'll need a set of pliers to remove any lodged quills and your dog won't be very cooperative. Consult your vet.

Rattlesnakes

Rattlesnakes can be a real hazard to dogs. When we hear the rattle, we know it means stay away. When your inquisitive buddy hears the rattle he thinks "Who can that be?" When hiking in rattlesnake country it is best to have Rover leashed. Rattlesnakes are a concern only on a few hikes in this book, particularly in the Blue Mountains and the Columbia Plateau. Consider visiting these areas during the cooler months when snake activity is minimal or absent. If your dog is bitten by a rattlesnake, immediately immobilize him. If you don't have antivenin for him, an antihistamine can be administered to stem swelling. Get your dog to a vet.

Bees

Dogs love to snap at them. If your buddy is stung, apply the same procedures that you would on yourself. Remove the stinger, ice if possible, and administer an antihistamine. Then try to avoid the urge to nap. Antihistamines always make me drowsy.

Ticks

Of far greater concern than bees are ticks. Ticks are the carriers of several diseases, some of which can be fatal to both you and your dog. Ticks are most prevalent in grazing areas, grassy areas, and open pine forests. They are most active in the spring, when they cling to the tips of tall grasses waiting for unsuspecting hosts to rub up against them. Fortunately it takes these little buggers a little time to march around and find the right spot, which on you is around your sock tops and waistline; and on your dog is her ears and snout. To avoid being ticked off, stay on the trail and avoid grassy areas. Do frequent body checks (on both of you). Ticks can usually be removed with tweezers. (Be sure to remove it at its head, close to the skin surface.) Topical canine applications such as Frontline do a decent job in repelling these little nuisances.

Range Country

Some of the hikes in this book, such as the Kettle Mountains, traverse areas of open range, where it is a good idea to keep your dog leashed.

Mittens spies a cow at Mount Leona trailhead.

Dogs that harass livestock can legally be shot. Cows generally won't hassle you. Keep your dog close by and wait for the bovines to disperse before proceeding. Some water sources may be contaminated in range areas, so keep your dog from drinking from them.

Hunting

Almost all of the areas covered in this book are open to hunting during the appropriate seasons. In heavily hunted regions such as the Blue Mountains and the Mallard-Larkins Area, it's best to avoid these trails during hunting season. When hiking during the late fall months keep your dog leashed (he can easily be mistaken for a deer) and wear orange. That goes for both of you. Orange cap and vest for you, orange vest for your dog. Don't take any chances—make sure you can be seen.

Using this Book

A guidebook is what the word describes: a book that guides. It is not meant to be inclusive or comprehensive. It does not replace the need to be responsible. It is my intent to introduce you to seventy-five of my favorite hikes in the Inland Northwest suitable for you and your dog. I've done the base work by walking all of the trails. Alan hiked them, too. And so did a dozen different dogs. I've noted places of interest, places of concern, and places of intrigue. I've noted, too, how to get to these places. But, alas, nothing remains constant. Things change, and that is why it is important that you contact relevant land agencies before setting out on any of these hikes. I've listed all of these within each hike's introduction.

What can change a hike? Trails can be affected by fires, floods, avalanches, and landslides. Sometimes land agencies open areas to resource extraction. Sometimes (and this is always a tragedy) land may be pulled from the public domain. Roads, too, change. They may degrade over time and become impassable. This is especially a concern in British Columbia where recent budgetary restraints have left the BC Forest Service with insufficient funds. Conversely, roads may improve, making it easier to get to some hikes. On the downside, this generally means more users.

Before setting out, along with contacting the appropriate land agencies, be sure to have appropriate maps. U.S. and Canadian topographic maps are good but are not always necessary if you plan to stick to popular trails. Good maps are often available for state and provincial parks, wildlife refuges, and federal wilderness areas. These maps, as well as forest service maps (both U.S. and BC), will make navigating easier.

The mileage for each hike is based on topographic maps. The noted distance indicates a round trip unless otherwise stated. Time estimates are just that, estimates. Some hikers and dogs will be quicker, others slower. The amount of time you take for breaks is up to you and your dog. The "best hiking times" that I have indicated were accomplished during snow-free periods. However, we Northwesterners know that some winters are mild and some never end! Hikes in the Okanagan Valley and the Columbia Plateau are dreadfully hot in the summer, so you'll notice that the best times mentioned for these areas are during cooler periods.

For Canada I have given distances in kilometers as well as miles because

Barkley peers out of an old lookout structure. (Photo by Craig Romano)

Canadian maps will be in kilometers. Also note that we did not make spelling errors in this book: In Canada, Kootenai is Kootenay; Okanogan is Okanagan; Yaak is Yahk. And remember that a loonie is not a crazy person but a dollar coin!

Any permits needed or special regulations are also listed in the introduction for each hike.

How the Trails Were Selected

Thousands of miles of trails within the Inland Northwest are open to dogs. So, how did I decide on these seventy-five hikes? While most trails permit dogs on them, they are not all necessarily good choices for dogs. My criteria for including trails in this book consisted of the following:

1. With few exceptions, I tried to avoid popular trails. I've included a few short hikes that are extremely popular with dog owners, trails that make for perfect first-time doggie hikes. Dogs who take to these popular trails should be comfortable with other dogs and hikers. I've offered alternative trails in popular areas, or alternative routes to popular destinations.

2. I've avoided trails that see a lot of mountain bike and/or motorized use. Only two trails in this guide are open to motorcycles, but their use is limited.

3. I've tried to avoid popular equestrian trails, but you should expect to encounter a few horses on a handful of these trails.

4. Most of the hikes in this guide go along rivers and creeks, and/or to lakes. It is extremely important to have plenty of water available for your pup.

5. Many of the trails are forested, offering comfortable hiking even on warm summer days.

6. I've tried to include trails that have an agreeable tread for your dog. I've stayed clear of rocky areas and areas that harbor prickly plants.

7. I've tried to provide hikes that will appeal to both you and your dog. Scenic views, old-growth forests, lush river valleys, sparkling lakes, and occasional summits.

8. When possible, trails originate from or near car-camping areas.

Are these hikes the absolute best places for taking your dog for a hike? Alan, Mittens, and I think so, but we know that there are a few other trails out there that we didn't include, trails that are equally "the best." This book isn't meant to be comprehensive. By all means we encourage you to seek out new trails. Meanwhile, enjoy the ones we have presented to you in this book. Happy hiking!

Enjoy the Trails: Get Involved

The trails in this book didn't materialize out of nowhere. But if we don't care for them and advocate for their protection, they may very well disappear into nowhere. If you want to get involved in building, maintaining, and/or advocating for our trails and the land they traverse, I encourage you to get involved with some of the groups listed below. Many of the lands covered in this book lack formal protection. Some places, such as the Kettle Mountains and the Upper Priest River valley, were excluded from past wilderness legislation. Other areas like the

Jax rests at Revett Lake. (Photo by Craig Romano)

Great Burn, Mallard-Larkins, and Cube Iron Mountains regions represent some of the last large roadless tracts in the Inland Northwest—and conservationists would like to see these areas designated as wilderness.

The Cascadians
P.O. Box 2201
Yakima, WA 98907
www.cascadians.org

Granby Wilderness Society
Box 2532
Grand Forks, BC V0H 1H0
(250) 442-2125
www.granbywilderness.org

Kettle Range Conservation Group
PO Box 150
Republic, WA 99166
(509) 775-2667 or the Spokane office, (509) 747-1663
www.kettlerange.org

Kootenay Mountaineering Club
Box 3195
Castlegar, BC V1N 3H5
www.kootenaymountaineering.bc.ca

Kootenay Columbia Trail Society
Box 1179
Rossland, BC V0G 1Y0
www.rosslandtrails.ca

The Lands Council
423 W. First Avenue, Suite 240
Spokane, WA 99201
(509) 838-4912
www.landscouncil.org

Northwest Ecosystem Alliance
1208 Bay Street #201
Bellingham, WA 98225
(360) 671-9950
www.ecosystem.org

Spokane Mountaineers Inc.
PO Box 1013
Spokane WA 99210
(509) 839-4974
www.spokanemountaineers.org

Washington Trails Association
1305 Fourth Avenue, Suite 512
Seattle, WA 98101
(206) 625-1367
www.wta.org

Western Canada Wilderness Committee
227 Abbott Street
Vancouver, BC V6B 2K7
(800) 661-9453
www.wildernesscommittee.org

A Note About Safety

Safety is an important concern in all outdoor activities. No guidebook can alert you to every hazard or anticipate the limitations of every reader. Therefore, the descriptions of roads, trails, routes, and natural features in this book are not representations that a particular place or excursion will be safe for your party. When you follow any of the routes described in this book, you assume responsibility for your own safety. Under normal conditions, such excursions require the usual attention to traffic, road and trail conditions, weather, terrain, the capabilities of your party, and other factors. Because many of the lands in this book are subject to development and/or change of ownership, conditions may have changed since this book was written that make your use of some of these routes unwise. Always check for current conditions, obey posted private property signs, and avoid confrontations with property owners or managers. Keeping informed on current conditions and exercising common sense are the keys to a safe, enjoyable outing.

The Mountaineers Books

PART 2

The Trails

OKANOGAN HIGHLANDS

1. Tiffany Mountain and Lake

Location: Okanogan Highlands
Round Trip: 10 miles
Hiking Time: 6 hours
High Point: 8242 feet
Elevation Gain: 1450 feet
Map: Green Trails Tiffany Mountain No. 53
Best Hiking Time: mid-June to mid-October
Contact: Okanogan National Forest, Tonasket Ranger District,
  (509) 486-2186

Driving Directions: From Winthrop, Washington, head north out of town on the East Chewuch River Road (County Road 9137). Five miles past the turnoff to Pearrygin Lake State Park turn right onto Forest Road 37. Follow FR 37 for 13 miles (pavement ends after mile 7), then bear left onto FR 39. Continue on FR 39 for 7.5 miles to Tiffany Spring

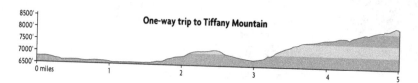

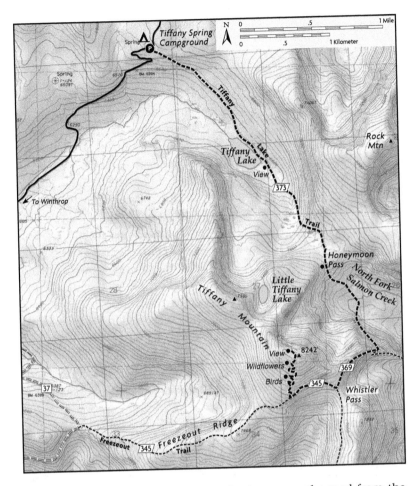

Campground. Tiffany Lake Trail 373 begins across the road from the campground at 6800 feet.

This hike is not the shortest nor the easiest route to Tiffany Mountain. Most hikers who head for the queen of the Okanogan Highlands opt for the much shorter Freezeout Ridge Trail. But what's the rush? By heading to the lofty summit of Tiffany via Tiffany Lake, you'll get to enjoy not only the broad open summit of the mountain, but also a lovely alpine lake and miles of lightly trampled trail.

You and your dog will get to romp on the shores of a pristine body of water, traverse lush forests, savor the floral aroma of alpine meadows, and soak up plenty of rays and views from a summit more than

Ollie rests on Tiffany Mountain summit. (Photo by Craig Romano)

8000 feet high. Because Tiffany sits on the extreme eastern edge of the Cascades, expect plenty of sunshine. However, when the Okanogan Valley begins to swelter and a front moves in, be prepared for an occasional thunderstorm. A sudden boom can produce a whimper—and your dog doesn't much appreciate thunder either.

The trail begins at the Tiffany Spring Campground, a lovely little spot with six sites at 6800 feet. Your vehicle did most of the climbing for you. Now you and your furry companion can stretch your legs and enjoy the high country. Tiffany Lake is reached in less than a mile, a pleasurable walk during which you'll lose about 100 feet in elevation. The lake, one of the largest in these parts, makes for a wonderful destination in its own right. However, lofty Tiffany Mountain, visible from the shore, beckons you.

Continue beyond the lake on Trail 373, through meadows and marshes. Climb a steady 500 feet to Honeymoon Pass, about 2.5 miles from the trailhead. This is free-range country so keep Rover nearby. Beyond Honeymoon Pass you'll drop into a lonely basin adorned with flowering plants and flowing streams. Cross the North Fork of Salmon Creek—a good place for a splash—then begin another 500-foot climb.

One mile from Honeymoon Pass you'll come to a junction with Trail 369. A small creek runs nearby, the last reliable water on the way to Tiffany Mountain. Turn right (southwest) and begin climbing 0.5 mile through a beautiful white-bark pine forest to Whistler Pass at 7600 feet. A weathered sign and cairns mark the junction with Freezeout Ridge Trail 345. Turn right (west) and follow this trail for 0.5 mile. The tread can be sketchy through the sprawling meadows, so keep a sharp eye to the ground.

You'll soon come to another signed junction. Trail 345 continues for 2.5 miles to FR 39. Turn right and head up the unmarked trail to the summit of Tiffany. In 0.5 mile and 500 feet of more climbing you and your dog will emerge panting on the 8242-foot summit. Views abound. The Pasayten country dominates the west, BC's Snowy Mountain can be seen in the north, the Kettle Range and Okanogan Valley spread across the eastern horizon, and the Beaver Meadow country occupies the view to the south.

Once you leave this alpine splendor, either return the 5 miles you came, or take the Freezeout Ridge Trail to FR 39, making this hike a loop and adding 1.5 miles. However, you'll have to walk the road 3.5 miles back to Tiffany Meadows. It's lightly traveled though, and there are lots of meadows and plenty of water along the way.

2. Snowshoe Meadow

Location: Okanogan Highlands
Round Trip: 12 miles
Hiking Time: 7–8 hours
High Point: 6400 feet
Elevation Gain: 1200 feet
Map: Green Trails Horseshoe Basin No. 21
Best Hiking Time: June through October
Contact: Washington State Department of Natural Resources, Colville, (DNR) (509) 684-7474

Driving Directions: From downtown Tonasket, Washington, look for a sign reading "Many Lakes Recreation Area, Loomis, Nighthawk." Turn here (west) following the Loomis Highway for 16 miles to tiny Loomis. Turn right (north) on County Road 9425 (Loomis-Oroville Road) and follow for 2 miles. Turn left on Forest Road 39 (Toats Coulee Road) and head west 7 miles to a V-intersection just beyond a cattle guard. Bear right (sign for Cold Springs Campground) onto a rough gravel road for 6.5 miles to Cold Springs Campground (bearing right at the first intersection, left at the second intersection, and left at the third

One-way trip to Snowshoe Meadow

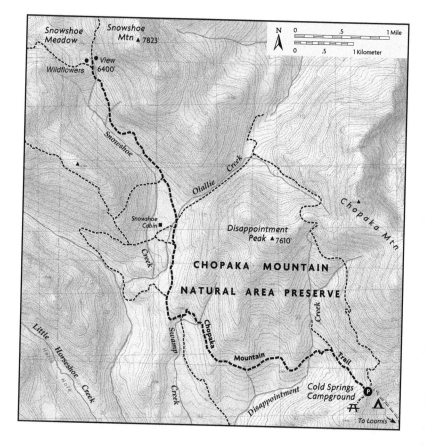

intersection). Just beyond the campground and before the entrance to a picnic area find trailhead parking on the right, at 6200 feet. The trail begins to the left (unmarked) on an old road leading downhill. (The gated road-trail that leads right goes to Disappointment Peak, Hike 3.)

Tucked along the Canadian border where the Cascades yield to the Okanogan Highlands is a wild and remote corner of the Evergreen State. Bordering the Pasayten Wilderness to the west and BC's Snowy Mountain Provincial Park to the north is the Loomis State Forest, a land of lofty open summits, thick pine forests, and deep lush valleys. Much of the northern reaches of this forest have been designated a Natural Resource Conservation Area (NRCA), meaning that it'll remain wild, just like its two neighbors.

But unlike its neighbors, especially the Pasayten, the Loomis sees very few visitors. Here's a hike up a lonely valley just 6 miles to the east of heavily traveled and hoofed Horseshoe Basin. And while a handful of equestrians choose the Snowshoe Meadow Trail as a backdoor entrance to Horseshoe Basin, most days only deer leave their footprints along this trail. Chances are very good that you and your dog will have this entire valley to yourselves, not counting all of the wild critters. Your dog will especially like sniffing out just *who* does reside here.

Spruce grouse in lodgepole pines, Loomis State Forest

The trails to Snowshoe Meadow receive very little maintenance. Furthermore, old roads and routes traverse the area, causing some route-finding confusion. It is imperative to carry a good map while hiking this route. You and your dog will be rewarded for any inconvenience you may encounter along the way.

The route to Snowshoe Meadow begins by following the Chopaka Mountain Trail (**Note:** This is NOT the trail up Chopaka. That is the Disappointment Peak route—see Hike 3). This good but unmarked trail leads west and downhill from the saddle where you begin, dropping 500 feet in 2 miles to Swamp Creek (5700 ft.). At Swamp Creek you'll intersect an old logging road. It is possible to access this point from the Fourteen Mile Trailhead, but it requires a long slog through a heavily logged area.

Follow the road north through cutover areas and eventually back to forest. After a short rise the road, now resembling a trail again, emerges along Olallie Creek. Just shy of 4 miles from the trailhead you'll come to a sometimes signed junction. The trail to the right leads 1.25 mile to the old mine road that goes over Disappointment Peak. A 9-mile loop is possible. For Snowshoe Meadow continue on the trail to the left, following the west fork of Olallie Creek.

Through dense forest and along the creek, this lightly used trail climbs 600 feet in 2 miles to Snowshoe Meadow (6400 ft.). Now deep in the Loomis backcountry the two of you have some options. Kick back and enjoy the meadow or set up camp for further explorations. Two trails head off from the meadows (they may be hard to find—perhaps your dog can sniff out the "trail apples" to find them). The one to the west heads 6 miles to Horseshoe Basin (very limited water). The one north goes 1.5 miles to the Canadian border. Don't cross the 10-foot-wide swath even if your dog is a Newfoundland or a Labrador; instead angle back south over open meadows and climb 7823-foot Snowshoe Mountain.

And, yes, there are snowshoe hares here! Your buddy has probably pointed that out to you already.

3. Disappointment Peak

Location: Okanogan Highlands
Round Trip: 5 miles
Hiking Time: 3 hours
High Point: 7160 feet
Elevation Gain: 1200 feet
Map: Green Trails Horseshoe Basin No. 21
Best Hiking Time: May through October
Contact: Washington State Department of Natural Resources, Colville, (DNR), (509) 684-7474

Driving Directions: From downtown Tonasket, Washington, look for a sign reading "Many Lakes Recreation Area, Loomis, Nighthawk." Turn here (west) following the Loomis Highway for 16 miles to tiny Loomis. Turn right (north) on County Road 9425 (Loomis-Oroville Road) and follow it for 2 miles. Turn left on Forest Road 39 (Toats Coulee Road) and head west 7 miles to a V-intersection just beyond a cattle guard. Bear right (sign for Cold Springs Campground) onto a rough gravel road for 6.5 miles to Cold Springs Campground (bear right at the first intersection, left at the second intersection, and left at the third intersection). Just beyond the campground and before the entrance to a picnic area you'll find trailhead parking on the right, at 6200 feet.

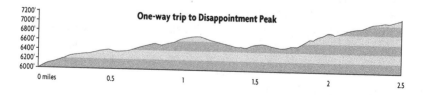

One-way trip to Disappointment Peak

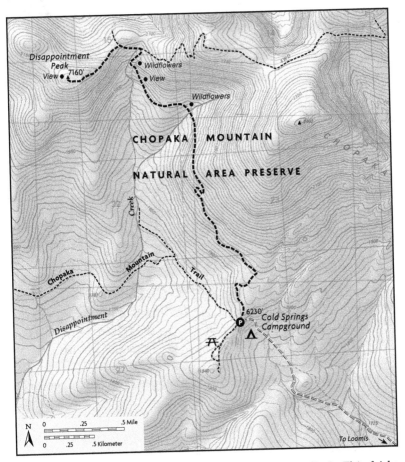

There's nothing disappointing about Disappointment Peak. This fairly easy hike is a great introduction to the wild and lonely Loomis State Forest, one of Washington's least known public lands. A few years back, much of the Loomis nearly succumbed to the chain saw. But, thanks to a well-funded and well-publicized campaign by a coalition of conservationists lead by the Northwest Ecosystem Alliance (NWEA), 25,000 acres of the Loomis State Forest has been reclassified as a Natural Resource Conservation Area (NRCA). All of this—sorry dogs—thanks to a cat! The high-elevation forests of the Loomis contain some of the best lynx habitat left in the Lower 48. The lynx is an elusive feline, so visiting dogs need not worry about being unwelcome.

The trail to Disappointment is actually an old mining road, gated and closed to all vehicles. With a trailhead elevation of over 6000 feet, you

Trail leading up slopes of Disappointment Peak

and Spot are granted easy entry into the Loomis high country. Follow the road-trail north into this special area. Much of the first half of the hike is through a mature lodgepole pine forest. These forests are prone to fire, clearly evident if you look out at the surrounding ridges, scarred and blackened.

After a short climb, the road-trail begins a gentle descent of about 200 feet into a lush boggy area. Signposts along the route here indicate that this microenvironment is within the Chopaka Mountain Natural Area Preserve. It is imperative that you and your dog stay on the trail so as not to disturb the myriad of rare plants growing here. More common plants growing here include sedges, moonworts, marsh marigolds, and wild strawberries.

After a mile you'll cross Disappointment Creek (6500 ft.), a great spot for admiring the small cascades and for your dog to play in them. Beyond the creek, you'll pass through a cool forest of Engelmann spruce and white-bark pine before emerging into an open meadow lined with sagebrush. The rest of the way to Disappointment Peak is up a southern sage-covered slope, which can get hot in July and August. Be sure to have adequate water for you and your pooch for the summit push.

Two miles from the start and 1 from the creek you'll come to a spring and a junction near a fence line (6850 ft.). The spring has been trampled by grazing cattle—best not to rely on it as a water source. The spring, however, is your clue to turn left onto the more obvious track. The track to the right leads 1 mile and 800 vertical feet up Joe Mills Mountain. For

strong hikers and dogs this is a side trip worth considering.
From the junction continue on the road-trail to a high saddle at 6950
feet. Do not follow the road down the north side of the ridge (the long
way to Snowshoe Meadow, Hike 2); instead leave the road west and follow the open ridge. It's a 10-minute stroll to the 7160-foot summit of
Disappointment Peak. The view provides a bird-dog's-eye view of the
Horseshoe Basin Peaks high country. To the east tower the Loomis Country giants: Chopaka Mountain, Joe Mills Mountain, and Hurley Peak.
Not bad country at all, even if it was set aside for a cat.

4. Fir Mountain

Location: Okanogan Highlands
Round Trip: 4 miles
Hiking Time: 4 hours
High Point: 5674 feet
Elevation Gain: 2150 feet
Map: USGS Wauconda Summit
Best Hiking Time: late June through mid-October
Contact: Okanogan National Forest, Tonasket Ranger District,
    (509) 486-2186

Driving Directions: From Tonasket, Washington, head east on State
Route 20 for 33 miles to Sweat Creek Picnic Area (From Republic,
Washington, travel west on SR 20 for 8 miles to Sweat Creek). Forest
Road 31 leaves south from SR 20 across from the picnic area. Drive FR
31 0.5 mile to the trailhead. The trail begins on the right, signed, "Fir
Mt Tr. No. 320." Park on the left-hand road shoulder. Parking is limited.

Long a favorite hike in the Okanogan Highlands, Mount Bonaparte has
sadly succumbed to dirt bikes and ATVs. What peace-loving hiker and
his dog would care to substitute the song of the thrush for that of the
throttle? Forget about Bonaparte. Across the high valleys and meadows

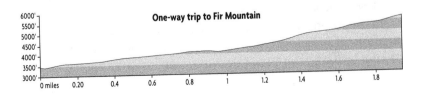

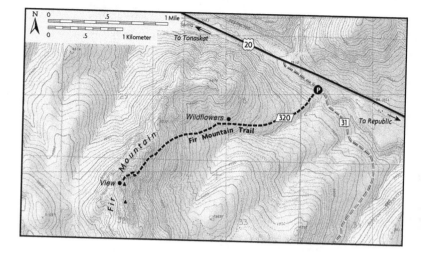

to the south is a righteous substitute: Fir Mountain. All but forgotten, the trail remains in good shape and nary a human soul uses it.

For those who venture to this forgotten corner of the Okanogan Highlands, solitude is guaranteed. So are fantastic views from an open summit of basalt. Big game is abundant in the forests and meadows, and a quiet hiker and dog should witness deer, bear, or elk.

The only drawback: Fir Mountain tends to be a dry place come midsummer. Pack plenty of fluids. Your poochie may be disappointed—the fir is Doug fir, not dog fur. However, many are quite old, even if measured in dog years!

The trail begins in a grassy area on a fading cat track (not that kind of cat!). Look for big larches with notches indicating course of direction. Within a few minutes, well-defined tread begins. Through a parklike open forest of Douglas fir, western larch, and ponderosa pine the trail works its way up the mountain. In 0.75 mile you'll come to a streambed, which is dry in late summer. If flowing, this is your last reliable water source.

The climb steepens and limited views through the forest preview the open basaltic ledges of the mountain's upper reaches. In about 1.25 miles the trail crosses an outcropping, and the views expand. Ten minutes later the trail crosses an opening of meadow and ledge. Look east for a fantastic view of the Kettle Mountain skyline.

The tread fades a little—look for cairns to guide you. The path gets a little steeper and a little creative, sneaking up, below, and around ledges. Short-legged dogs may need help. The final push to the summit is along an open ledge. Use caution. Keep your dog nearby if he likes to wander. Emerge on the broad, open summit. Find the fire keep's old outhouse (your dog will probably point it out), and explore extended ridges. Be careful around the site of the lookout tower—glass and nails don't make good souvenirs for your dog's foot pads.

Soak up the panoramic view: the entire Kettle Crest from Togo to Grizzly Peak to the east; Omak and Moses mountains to the south; the Tiffany Highlands to the west; and White and Baldy to the north. There are great views, too, of Bonaparte, quite peaceful from this vantage point.

Sailor plays with a pinecone along the trail.

5. Swan Lake and Butte

Location: Okanogan Highlands
Round Trip: 2.3 miles
Hiking Time: 2 hours
High Point: 3825 feet
Elevation Gain: 175 feet
Map: USGS Aeneas
Best Hiking Time: May through October
Contact: Colville National Forest, Republic Ranger District, (509) 775-3305
Note: Dogs must be leashed in the campground and are not allowed on the beach.

Driving Directions: From Republic, Washington, head south on State Route 21 for 7 miles. Turn right (west) onto Forest Road 53 (also known as Scatter Creek Road and signed "Swan Lake 7 miles"). Follow this good paved road for 6.5 miles to the Swan Lake Campground. Proceed another 0.4 mile to the day-use area. The trail begins from the picnic area.

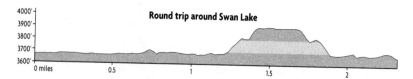

Are you looking for a quiet little retreat for you and your dog? A place where the two of you can go on a short hike before or after a day of swimming, fishing, and paddling? A snug lakeside campsite? Look no further than Swan Lake, a tranquil little body of water located in the rolling forested hills above the Sanpoil River valley.

The hike around the lake is only 1.5 miles. Add the trip to Swan Butte and you still have a pretty short hike. However, this loop isn't meant to be done quickly. The lake and surrounding forest teem with wildlife, and in the late evening or early morning you and your dog will be captivated by a flurry of activity. Mittens was completely mesmerized by the loons, not quite sure what to make of their eerie cries echoing over the placid waters.

Begin your hike from the picnic area, where you'll find a beautiful kitchen shelter constructed by the Civilian Conservation Corps. The trail travels along the shoreline, which ranges from ledgy to marshy. Look for moose tracks in the marshes; better yet, look for moose. Huckleberry bushes and big ponderosa pines line the way from time to time.

About halfway around the lake you'll come to the side trail that leads to Swan Butte. Follow this 0.4-mile path to the 3825-foot point. Although

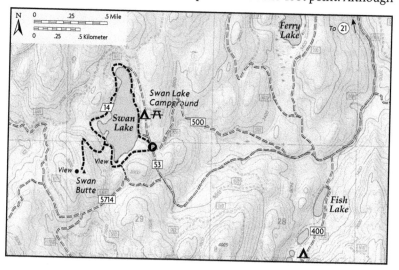

Katie on the shore of Swan Lake

you won't get much of a view of the lake from here, you will get a nice view of the Kettle Crest and the Thirteen Mile Creek peaks to the east.

Once you've finished soaking up views, return to the lake and complete the loop. Dogs are not allowed on the campground beach or in the day-use area. But anywhere away from those areas is fine. The lake warms up nicely by late summer.

CANADIAN OKANAGAN AND BOUNDARY COUNTRY

6. Wildhorse Canyon

Location: Okanagan Highlands
Round Trip: 11.5 miles (18.5 km)
Hiking Time: 6–7 hours
High Point: 2145 feet
Elevation Gain: 825 feet
Maps: Okanagan Mountain Provincial Park, 82 E/12 Summerland, 82 E/13 Peachland
Best Hiking Time: April to June, late September through November
Contact: BC Parks-Okanagan Regional Office, (250) 490-8200

Driving Directions: From Kelowna, British Columbia, turn off BC 97 (Harvey Ave) south onto Pandosy Street (second light after Floating Bridge if coming from the west). After 2 miles (2.5 km) Pandosy becomes Lakeshore Road. Continue on Lakeshore for 8 miles (13 km) to the

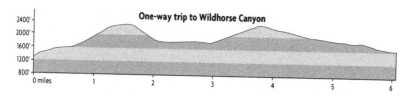

One-way trip to Wildhorse Canyon

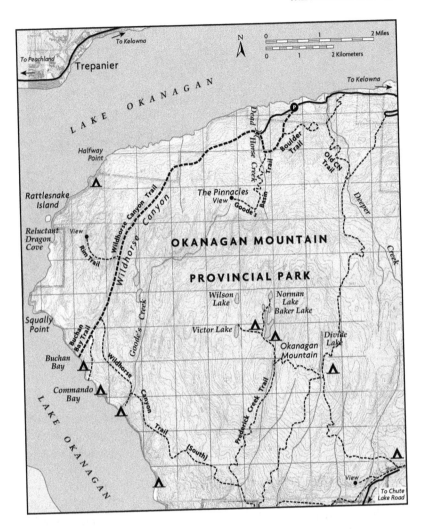

entrance of Okanagan Mountain Provincial Park. Continue on a gravel road past the main parking area for another mile. On your right (west) will be a tall relay tower. Look for an iron-gated old road directly across on your left (east)—this is the trailhead. It is easy to miss. Park on the shoulder. (Ignore old maps that show the trail beginning from the end of the road—this is private property.)

Much of the Okanagan Valley has succumbed to orchard, vineyard, and settlement during the past 100 years. It's quite surprising then that the

Angel rests in Wildhorse Canyon.

wildest remaining lands in this valley sit a mere 10 miles away from the region's largest city. Okanagan Mountain Provincial Park protects over 25,000 acres (10,400 hectares) of old-growth forests, craggy peaks, grassy ledges, and pristine lakeshore. It's an incredibly wild place—and one of the best for you and your dog to explore in the Okanagan Valley.

Almost 20 miles of trails traverse this park. The one through Wildhorse Canyon makes for an ideal early- or late-season hike, before the blistering heat of summer or the frigid freeze of winter. Most of this trail follows the original route of the fur-trading brigades of the mid-nineteenth century. It almost became a provincial highway, but local activists convinced government officials to preserve this historic trail. In 1973 the park was established. Now instead of sharing this route with buzzing semis and overstuffed SUVs, it'll be just you, your pooch, and a whole lot of wild critters.

Wildhorse Canyon is prime cougar country, so keep your dog nearby. This is one cat that has an edge when it comes to a showdown with your canine, though it is highly unlikely that you will encounter one. Ticks, on the other hand, are plentiful, so make sure you and Spot stay out of the high grasses that line the trail and the lakeshore. Water is plentiful along this trail, a real bonus in arid Okanagan Country.

The trail starts out on a semi-open slope with good views of massive Okanagan Lake and the little city of Peachland perched on its shore. Where the devastating wildfire of 2003 spared a grove, old ponderosa pines and Douglas firs provide shade. The open areas along this section teem with ground squirrel and quail. Old news to your dog— she's probably been alert to the riled rodents and cavorting coveys for some time now.

After 0.75 mile you'll come to a well-signed junction. Continue right, cross Dead Horse Creek on a sturdy bridge, then begin an uphill grunt. The trail, which follows an old road here, is eroded. Hang in there, it only gets better. A quarter mile from the creek the terrain levels off and you'll come to a junction with the Boulder Trail, an interesting side trip. Your route remains straight ahead, however. After another series of short, steep climbs the trail enters Wildhorse Canyon (2 miles), a classic canyon out of the wild west: rocky, craggy, and narrow. It's not dry, however, for this giant cleft through Okanagan Mountain Park has trapped plenty of precious precipitation. A string of shallow ponds line and nourish the canyon floor, providing an emerald swath through the gray chasm. Giant cottonwoods ring the wetlands. Waterfowl, woodpeckers, and amphibian life are prolific. Unfortunately so are mosquitoes. For a mesmerizing 3 miles, the same trail that brought fur trappers, cattlemen, and gold seekers to the Okanagan traverses this lovely and wild canyon. In early season keep your eyes peeled for big white critters on the canyon walls— mountain goats looking for a spring morsel or two. In late season those same canyon walls will dazzle your eyes as the golden aspens glisten.

In 4 miles you come to the junction with the Rim Trail. This side trail climbs out of the canyon into a rugged world of open forest and clefts. A series of small ponds (in early season) provides water. It's an option, but the better choice is to continue through Wildhorse Canyon to Okanagan Lake. In 4 miles leave the canyon and enter a beautiful forest of giant ponderosa pines. Come to another junction. The Wildhorse Canyon Trail continues left for over 7 miles to the south parking lot. You and your dog are better off proceeding right on the Buchan Bay Trail for a 1-mile trip to the lake, where you will find an inviting beach to rest and relax, or a place to overnight. Camping is allowed here. After all, trappers, voyageurs, and First Peoples have spent the night on this quiet cove for ages.

7. Myra Canyon

Location: Okanagan Highlands
Round Trip: 12 miles (19 km)
Hiking Time: 7 hours
High Point: 3960 feet
Elevation Gain: 300 feet
Maps: 82 E/14 Kelowna, 82 E/11 Wilkinson Creek
Best Hiking Time: late April to November
Contact: BC Parks-Okanagan Regional Office, (250) 490-8200
Note: This area was severely damaged by the 2003 Kelowna fires, causing park and trail closures. Burnt bridges and trestles are being replaced, but check with authorities before visiting to make sure the trail is open.

Driving Directions: From Kelowna, British Columbia, turn off BC 97 (Harvey Ave) right (south) onto Gordon Drive. Proceed for 1 mile, then turn left (east) onto K.L.O. Road. Follow K.L.O. for 2.5 miles to where it ends at a junction with East Kelowna Road and McCulloch Road near the East Kelowna Community Centre. Bear right onto McCulloch (follow signs for Myra Canyon) and follow this road 5 miles, passing Gallagher Canyon, to the Myra FS Road. Turn right on Myra (signed "Myra Canyon Trestles 8 km"), proceeding 5.25 miles to the trailhead (15 miles from Kelowna).

This is one of the most popular hikes in the Kelowna area. It's a social outing rich in history and scenic splendor. There'll be plenty of other dogs with their owners waiting to share the trail with you. This trail is admired by bicyclists, too, but not the mad bombers. It's mostly families putting along, gasping at the scenery. Early and late season are good times to visit if your pup is a little shy. It's advisable to keep him on a leash, even if he is well-behaved around other people, because the trestles are hazardous, especially for smaller, pug-size dogs. Prepare for one of the supreme hikes of the Okanagan Highlands.

The trip to Myra Canyon utilizes the old Kettle Valley Railroad line.

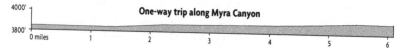

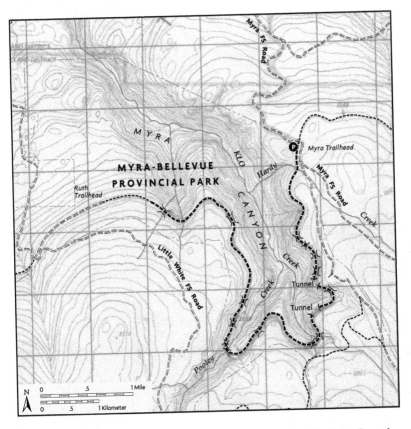

One of the most expensive and difficult lines ever to be built in Canada, it was abandoned in the 1960s. Converted to trail, the 6.2-mile (10 km) section through Myra Canyon is perhaps the most stunning section on the entire route. Within this short stretch the trail rounds the large horseshoe canyon by way of eighteen trestles and two tunnels. Maintaining an elevation of around 3800 feet, there are breathtaking views of the Okanagan Valley and Lake Okanagan all along the way. There are spectacular views, too, of rushing streams crashing below and big broad mountains rising above. Interpretive plaques give you a better understanding of the human history of this fascinating place. Your pup probably won't be interested in the interpretation, but she'll enjoy sniffing about in the seeps and clefts that line the trail.

Begin in a forest of lodgepole pine and aspen. Within 5 minutes you'll be greeted by views. Each kilometer is marked by a concrete post. Most of the trail and trestle rehabilitation was done by a volunteer group, the

One of several train trestles in Myra Canyon (Photo by Craig Romano)

Myra Canyon Trestle Restoration Society. Most of the wildlands that you're traversing are now part of the Myra-Bellevue Provincial Park, a 19,000-acre preserve established in the spring of 2004.

In 0.6 mile (1 km) you'll come to the first trestle. Enjoy the sweeping views across the canyon. Pick out the trestles nestled along the slopes. In 1.2 miles (2 km) you'll come to the first tunnel, and the second tunnel 0.6 mile (1 km) further. No lights are necessary—the tunnels are short.

Keep your eyes open, for there is much to see. Although the railroad opened up this area many years ago, today it is quite wild. Moose, bear, and cougars all frequent the canyon. Your dog will probably notice the smaller critters, such as the copious ermine and the pika.

At about 4 miles you'll come to the twelfth trestle, the longest in the canyon. It spans more than 700 feet, nearly 200 feet above the rushing creek below. This is a good spot to turn around if the complete canyon hike is too long. From this point the terrain gets less interesting and the remaining trestles are farther apart. If you carry on to the last trestle (6 miles), however, you'll enjoy a fantastic view back of the entire canyon and all of the area that you just traversed. This is a good lunch spot, too. If you want to continue to the old Ruth Rail Station site, it's roughly 1 mile further. The walking is easy but there's not much to look at. Turn around and have fun recrossing all the trestles. You're sure to meet new hikers and dogs on the way back to your vehicle.

8. Collier Lakes

Location: Okanagan Highlands
Round Trip: 3 miles (5 km)
Hiking Time: 2 hours
High Point: 4100 feet
Elevation Gain: 600 feet
Map: 82 E/7 Almond Mountain
Best Hiking Time: late April to November
Contact: British Columbia Ministry of Forests, Arrow Lake and
   Boundary District, Castlegar Ranger Station, (250) 365-8600

Driving Directions: From Kelowna, British Columbia, head south on BC 33 for 51 miles (82 km) towards the small hamlet of Beaverdell. One mile (2 km) before approaching Beaverdell, turn left on paved Beaver Creek Road. If approaching from the south, the turnoff is 30.5 miles (49 km) from the junction of BC 3 and BC 33 in Rock Creek.

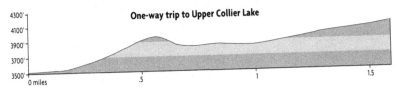

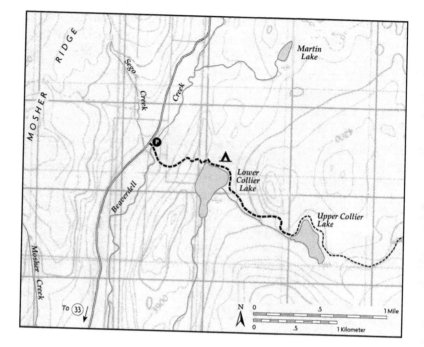

Follow Beaver Creek Road 4.5 miles (7 km) to a Y-junction. Bear right and continue for 6.2 miles (10 km). Just beyond kilometer-post 17 find the Sego Creek Campground. The trail begins just to the left of the information sign.

This is a short, sweet hike to two of the many little lakes that dot the high plateau separating the Kettle and West Kettle Rivers. This is a region that calls out to be explored by you and your poochie. Consider setting up camp at Sego Creek (be sure to get a camping permit, available at any forest district office), a lovely spot in its own right.

From the Sego Creek Campground it's a mere 0.6 mile (1 km) to the lower Collier Lake. But it's no easy half mile. For soon after entering the forest and crossing Malone Creek the trail gets down to business, proving once again that switchbacks are a rare commodity in BC. A steep little climb over a wooded ridge followed by a short little descent will soon bring you to the outlet of lower Collier.

It's a pretty spot, but continue on, crossing the outlet on a boardwalk to a small rise above the lake. Here you'll find a very inviting backcountry campsite surrounded by big firs and larches. Good lake access, too. The resident loons will probably startle your pup with their eerie calls. The mergansers, sandpipers, and canvasbacks will probably be startled by you two.

Lower Collier Lake is surrounded by grassy marshes. Scan them for moose. Your pal has probably already gotten his nose into the nuggets—they're all over the place here. He'll probably sniff up some bear evidence, too.

Beyond the campsite the trail continues 1 mile (1.5 km) to the upper lake. It is a most enjoyable hike, with very little elevation gain through a parklike setting of larch, pine, and aspen. The upper lake is a bit more shallow than the lower, but to your dog it's still inviting.

Consider this hike in the early season before the mosquitoes arrive, or later in the season when the larch and aspen add a golden touch to the lakes' tranquil shorelines.

Mittens at the shore of Lower Collier Lake

9. Thimble Mountain

Location: Okanagan Highlands
Round Trip: 7.5 miles
Hiking Time: 4 hours
High Point: 4300 feet
Elevation Gain: 700 feet
Map: 82 E/1 Grand Forks
Best Hiking Time: late April to June, September to November
Contact: British Columbia Ministry of Forests, Arrow Lake and
  Boundary District, Castlegar Ranger Station, (250) 365-8600

Driving Directions: From the junction of BC 3 and BC 21 in Grand
Forks, British Columbia, drive west 10.5 miles on BC 3. Turn right on a
gravel road at a large sign posted "Thimble Mountain Trails." In 0.25
mile turn left and follow this gravel road 0.75 mile to a junction. Turn
right and proceed 0.6 mile to trailhead. The trail will be on your right
(marked by a big information board) next to old mining structures (maps
may show as "BC Mines"). Park in the pull-out on the north side (left)
of the road.

The Thimble Mountain trails are perfect for an early-season or fall hike.
The snow melts early here and the weather is almost always good. Grand
Forks prides itself as being the sunshine capital of BC. But with all that
sun comes heat. In summer, Thimble Mountain is bone-dry (we're not
talking dog bones here) and this hike can be a scorcher. But when the
mercury settles in around 15° (that's Celsius—we're in Canada, remember?)
and a dry breeze drifts down from the Granby Valley, oh, what a
joy it is to ramble on these trails!

Study the reader board before heading out. The trail system can be
confusing. Just keep note of junctions and the two of you should be fine.

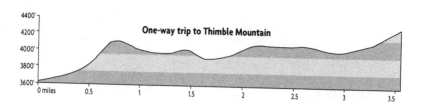

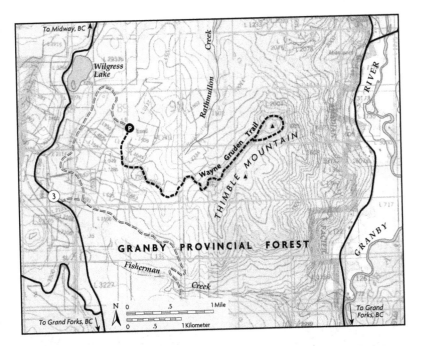

Begin on an old road marked by orange tags. After 0.5 mile the route becomes a real trail. Through open forest and grassy meadows, begin climbing the south slopes of Thimble. To the south the Kettle Mountains come into view. After about 1.5 miles you'll come to an old skid road where you turn right (signed for Thimble). Shortly afterwards, in a cedar grove, the trail leaves the skid road, going left (signed).

Through open forest the going is easy. After 2.5 miles you'll come to a fence line and a trail junction (signed). Bear left (straight), veering away from the fence line. Water is sometimes available in a nearby depression. In 3 miles you come to another old road junction, where you turn right. Immediately afterwards, a sign promising a viewpoint directs you to turn left. This is the Wayne Gruden Trail, the literal and figurative high point of this hike.

The Gruden Trail makes a loop around the summit ledges of Thimble. I prefer doing the loop clockwise to build up momentum for the views. The level trail cuts through a dry forest with lots of open ledges. While you scan the horizon, your pooch will be preoccupied with the unlimited grouse that call this peak home. In 3.75 miles you'll come to a large series of basaltic ledges. Prepare for the granddaddy view of the Granby Valley.

Keep your buddy close by, for it's quite a drop off the ledge. Two-thousand feet below, the Granby River snakes and oxbows through a valley of pastoral farms. To the east, Gladstone and Faith Peaks rise above steep forested ridges. The Kettle Crest spans the southern horizon.

Once you're ready to commence hiking, continue another 0.75 mile to close the loop. It's 3 miles back to your vehicle via the way you came. You can always extend this hike by rambling on some of the other loops that veer off to the southeast, but it is advisable to do this only if there is snowmelt for water.

Beta the Brittany spaniel rests along the trail.

10. Granby River

Location: Boundary Country
Round Trip: 21 miles (34 km)/Granby Canyon: 10 miles (16 km)
Hiking Time: 2 days/Granby Canyon: 5 hours
High Point: 3000 feet (Granby Canyon)
Elevation Gain: 200 feet
Maps: 82 E/8 Deer Park, E/9 Burrell Creek
Best Hiking Time: May to November
Contact: BC Parks-Okanagan Regional Office, (250) 490-8200

Driving Directions: From Grand Forks, British Columbia, head east on BC 3. Just beyond the Granby River Bridge turn left onto the Granby River Road. Follow this road north. The pavement ends in 27 miles (43 km) at the 28 Mile Bridge. Cross Burrell Creek. Continue on a good gravel road (watch for logging trucks). A half mile from the bridge, bear left at a junction; then bear right at another junction 2.5 miles further. Six miles beyond the second junction (Gable Creek Road) you come to an intersection with Blue Joint Road. Turn right on Blue Joint and proceed for 1 mile to a rough road that branches left. Here, 37 miles from Grand Forks, a sign for Granby Park points left. Park far on the shoulder of Blue Joint and proceed by foot down the rough Traverse Creek Road. A footbridge crosses the oft swift-flowing Howe Creek. If you have a four-wheel drive it's possible to cross the creek and drive to the official trailhead 2.5 miles beyond.

A major tributary to the Kettle River, wild and pristine Granby flows down from the rugged Monashee Mountains. This is the dry BC southern interior, a region sparsely populated but heavily exploited. Miners and loggers have left their marks. But the upper reaches of the Granby watershed are still wild and intact. Boundless tracts of old-growth forest, sprawling alpine meadows, and an untamed river are all protected within the Granby

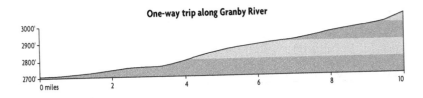

One-way trip along Granby River

Provincial Park. Although a handful of interior grizzlies still roam this 100,000-acre preserve, encounters with the great bears are rare. An encounter with a great river, however, awaits all who walk this way. You and your dog will be captivated and mesmerized by this magical waterway.

Trails are rare in Granby Park (most are old miners' and trappers' routes), but thanks to the Granby Wilderness Society, the Granby River Trail is well-maintained and easy to follow. It's getting to the trailhead that's a challenge. Because the Howe Creek crossing is impossible for most vehicles, most hikers will have to walk 2.5 miles along the access road before getting to the trail. That's not a bad thing though, for this riverside road is quiet and scenic. Plenty of dispersed campsites exist in the open lodgepole pine forests that line the way. In 1.5 miles you'll come to an information kiosk. One mile further the "road" ends at a small campground

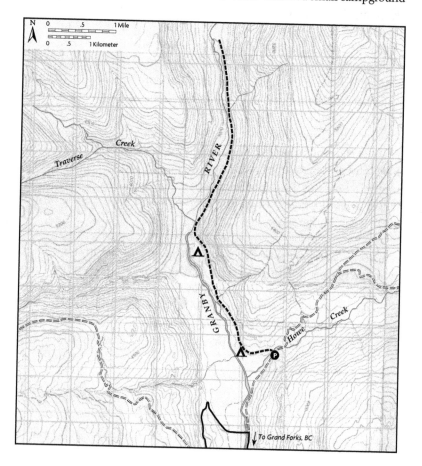

Mittens wades the icy waters of the Granby River.

in a beautiful cedar grove. This is the official beginning of the trail.

Most of the way is easy going, but a short section through the impressive Granby Canyon may require an extra helping hand for your furry friend. Keep her close by here, for there are some steep drops.

Through giant larches, cedars, fir and pines, the trail heads into the Granby wilderness. In this "dry interior" ecosystem, water is never a problem. The river is always nearby and plenty of creeks feed it along the way.

One mile from the campground and 3.5 miles from the start, you'll enter the canyon. The often-hidden river makes its way over and around giant boulders and cascades through a narrow, rocky chasm, like a southern Appalachian river. Watch your footing here. Short-legged pooches will need a boost or two.

After nearly 2 miles of spectacular canyon hiking, the trail emerges on a high bench and the route gets easier. Watch for moose as you pass a series of bogs. Finally, after 3.5 miles of trail (6 miles from the start), you'll enter the provincial park. From this point on it's nothing but true wilderness.

Continue for as far as you like. The trail travels up and down over bluffs, hugs the riverfront, and provides plenty of places along the way to soak feet or throw down a tent.

Rocky outwashes make good sunning posts while sandy coves make good places to soak. The trail eventually fades at 8 miles (10.5 miles from the starting point). Travel beyond that point is for experienced hikers and hounds only. For most intrepid pairs, a hike to the canyon and back will be rewarding enough.

11. Deer Point-Christina Lake

Location: Boundary Country
Round Trip: 14 miles (22.5 km)
Hiking Time: 8 hours
High Point: 2000 feet
Elevation Gain: (and loss) 400 feet
Map: 82 E/1 Grand Forks
Best Hiking Time: April to November
Contact: BC Parks-Okanagan Regional Office, (250) 490-8200
Note: Dogs need to be leashed and are not allowed on beaches at Texas Creek.

Driving Directions: From Castlegar, British Columbia, drive west on BC 3 for 41 miles (65 km). Look for a sign announcing "Gladstone Provincial Park-Texas Creek Campground." The road is on your right, but you must make a left turn (turning lane and jug handle access) to safely approach this intersection. Cross BC 3 and proceed 3 miles (5 km) on East Lake Drive to the provincial park boundary. Unless camping, park outside of the gate on the right. If coming from the east, the park turnoff is 6.2 miles (10 km) from the junction of BC 3 and BC 395.

Big, beautiful Christina Lake—you won't get tired of looking at it. And with some of the warmest waters in all of Canada, your buddy won't get tired of playing in it. Cottages line the southern third of the 6500-acre lake, but the northern two-thirds is protected within the ecologically important Gladstone Provincial Park. Recently expanded in 2004, the park now contains over 97,000 acres of some of the best grizzly habitat remaining within the southern interior of the province. It's highly un-likely that you and your dog will encounter a grizzly, but black bears are quite common. Be sure that ol' Spot stays by your side.

The hike to Deer Point takes you to the wild, north end of Christina Lake. It makes for a good early-season hike when the surrounding high country is still buried in snow. In summer the hike entices, too, with those

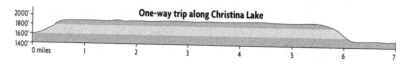

One-way trip along Christina Lake

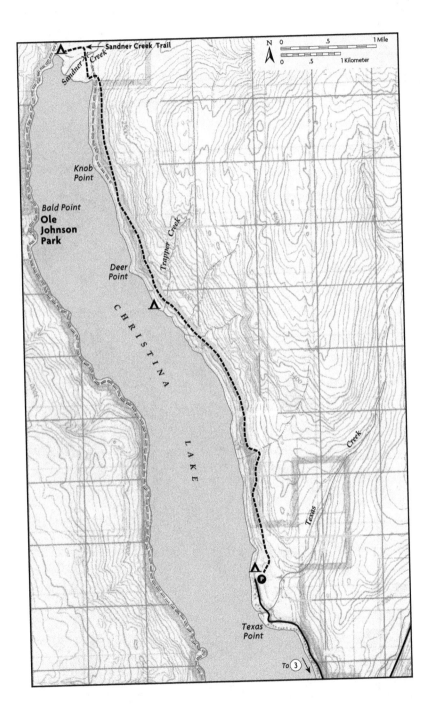

refreshing lake waters awaiting you at Deer Point. However, although the trail travels along Christina's shore, most of the time you are high above it. It can get hot here in July and August, so pack plenty of water for the two of you while en route to all the water you could possibly want.

The trail to Deer Point begins from the Texas Creek Campground just past site 42 (water and restrooms available). Through a forest of ponderosa pine and Douglas fir the trail begins to climb. In spring, blossoming syringa whiten the dense understory. After 10 minutes you come to a side trail leading to a view of the lake. Climb for another 15 minutes, then relax as the trail flattens out on a bench above the lake.

Ferns and birches line the way, reminiscent of eastern Canada. In 2 miles there is a creek crossing, most likely dry by late summer. Shortly afterwards the forest opens up, providing you with a knockout view of Christina. This spot makes for a good turnaround for a shorter hike.

Continue along the high bench, crossing open bluffs that allow you to soak up the sun as well as the scenery. In 3.5 miles you'll come to the Trapper Creek campsite. Unfortunately the creek usually isn't flowing.

In 5.5 miles you'll get a view of Deer Point. Now begin a steep descent as you leave the bench and get closer to that lake you've been admiring for miles. First you'll reach an old, fading road, the Sandner Creek Trail, a lonely route into the heart of the park. Continue left, and at 6 miles leave the heat and enter a cool cedar grove gracing Sandner Creek. Finally some water! Cross the creek on a log bridge and round the northern tip of the lake following the trail to the Troy Creek Campground at Deer Point. Here, 7 miles from the trailhead, is your own private beach (with maybe a canoeist or two). Your dog will probably be in the soothing waters before you even take your pack off.

If you find it hard to leave this heavenly spot, there's probably room to throw your tent down. Just be sure to register at Texas Creek before setting out.

Opposite: Ghiry rests in camp at Deer Point along the shores of Christina Lake. (Photo by Craig Romano)

CANADIAN KOOTENAY REGION

12. Record Ridge

Location: Kootenay Country
Round Trip: 5 miles (8 km)
Hiking Time: 3 hours
High Point: 6100 feet
Elevation Gain: 1600 feet
Map: 82 F/4 Rossland-Trail
Best Hiking Time: late May through October
Contact: British Columbia Ministry of Forests, Arrow Lake and Boundary District, Castlegar Ranger Station, (250) 365-8600

Driving Directions: From Trail, British Columbia, head west on BC 3B for 7 miles (11 km) to the junction with BC 22 in the alpine town of Rossland. Turn left on BC 22, proceeding for .25 mile. Immediately across from the Rossland Motel turn right onto Rossland-Cascade Road and follow it for 7 miles (12 km) to the height of land just beyond power lines and a buried gas line. Park on either side of road. Find the signpost for Record Ridge on the west side.

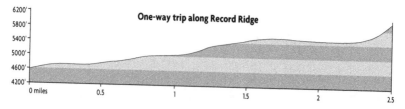

One-way trip along Record Ridge

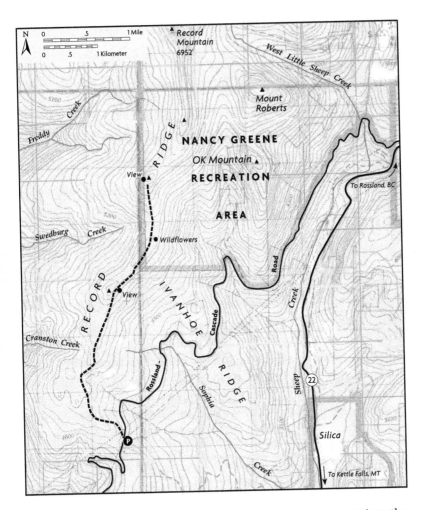

The hike up Record Ridge offers a much easier and shorter route into the highlands of the Rossland Range than the trip up Old Glory (Hike 13). You'll still get far-reaching views, wildflower-filled meadows, and a prime backcountry experience, but without all the work. And even though this hike is short and close to the outdoor recreation town of Rossland, it doesn't see much use. Most of Rossland's active visitors come to mountain bike, and there are plenty of trails better for biking than this one.

Although the hike to Record Ridge can be enjoyed throughout the summer and fall, it's best to avoid it during heat spells. The entire approach is along a southern slope, mostly open and mostly dry. Plan accordingly or the both of you will be panting dearly. You're up high enough

Characteristic grassy meadow along Record Ridge

not to have to worry about rattlesnakes, but note that the Rossland Range is prime bear habitat, both black and griz.

The trail begins steeply on an old road and soon veers left through a grassy area. Be sure to watch for signposts and bright orange squares marking the route. After about 10 minutes the route makes a sharp right and becomes an actual trail. It's a steep little climb through open forest and over grassy ledges. Views begin and only get better. If you lose the way in the grassy areas just look for cairns.

After about 0.5 mile you'll pass a small relay tower and enter a cool forest of lodgepole pine and larch, a welcome reprieve from the sun. In about 1.25 miles the way really opens up, with extensive views of Washington's Selkirk and Kettle River ranges. Enjoy the floral show at your feet. There are old mining pits scattered about so keep your pooch nearby. It's probably best not to let her drink from the stagnant pools that have collected in some of them.

The grade eases to a splendid ridge walk with sweeping views. Glacial erratics lie scattered about. The trail rounds the ridge to the left and makes one last short, steep climb to attain a rocky and open high point (6100 ft.) at 2.5 miles. It's possible to continue along the ridge cross-country, but only sure-footed hikers and canines should attempt this.

Otherwise, scamper around this rocky knoll and take in the awesome views of the deep Sheep Creek Valley to the west and little Rossland to the east. Sunsets are spectacular from up here and the trail is short enough to consider it.

13. Old Glory

Location: Kootenay Country
Round Trip: 11 miles (17.5 km)
Hiking Time: 7 hours
High Point: 7844 feet
Elevation Gain: 3300 feet
Map: 82 F/4 Rossland-Trail
Best Hiking Time: July to early October
Contact: Contact: British Columbia Ministry of Forests, Arrow Lake and Boundary District, Castlegar Ranger Station, (250) 365-8600

Driving Directions: From the junction of BC 22 and BC 3B in Rossland, British Columbia, drive west on BC 3B for 6.25 miles (10 km). On the left side of the road (south) is a small pull-off that is easy to miss. Look for an elongated post signed "Old Glory Trail." There's parking for three vehicles here; a pull-off across the highway will accommodate three more.

Old Glory is the granddaddy of the Rossland Range. At nearly 8000 feet it provides spectacular views ranging from the Cascades and the Kettles in the west to the Selkirks in the east and the Monashee Mountains to the north—a sea of green punctuated by icy toppings. The hike is demanding, but by making a loop that utilizes Unnecessary Ridge the climb is softened.

You and your dog should be experienced hikers and in good physical shape before reveling in Old Glory. Water is not a problem, but most of the high country is open and exposed. In hot or inclement weather there's

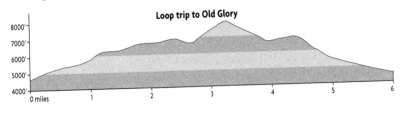

Loop trip to Old Glory

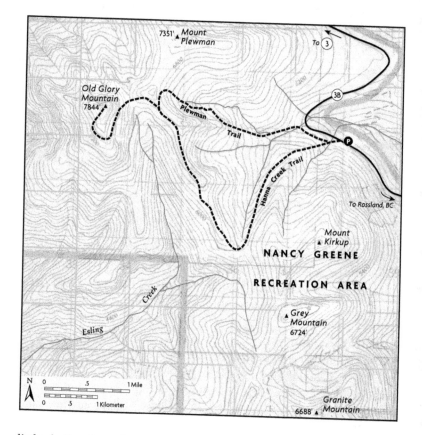

little shelter. Snow lingers on the summit well into July. Although the summit block is broad and grassy, the north and east faces contain steep cliffs, so keep your furry friend close by.

Old Glory and particularly Big Sheep Creek basin to the south is home to a couple of grizzlies. A few wolverines, too. Although it is highly unlikely that you'll encounter these critters, caution should be exercised. Keep Rover by your side and be aware of any recent activity, such as overturned clumps of meadow or fresh tracks. With the proper precautions, you'll enjoy this hike, one of the most spectacular in this book.

The hike begins immediately in a dense old-growth forest reminiscent of the Cascades. In the giant cedars and hemlock you'll soon encounter a junction. The Plewman Trail, your return, takes off right. Continue left on the Hanna Creek Trail, which utilizes an old road. On a generally good path—a few eroded areas here and there—the route traverses mature and second-growth forests as it heads for the ridge. Rushing creeks abound.

In 2 miles (3 km) you'll come to a four-way intersection, where you go right. With a good portion of climbing now under your buddy's leash it's time to enjoy the easy grade along Unnecessary Ridge. Through thinning forest and along granite ledges and wildflower-saturated meadows the Rossland Range high country unfolds. At about 3 miles (5 km) you'll get your first view of Old Glory, its old lookout precipitously perched on its northern flank.

The way opens up even more. Enter a world of swaying grasses, dancing flowers, and whistling silver snags. The broad, glacially carved Big Sheep Creek basin spreads out directly below. After 2 miles of glorious ridge hiking and 4 miles (6.5 km) from the start you come to the Plewman Trail junction. That is your departure course for this hike, but first Old Glory's summit must be attained, 2 miles away.

The trail to Old Glory drops 250 feet off the ridge to contour around the summit block from the south. En route you'll pass through a high basin ringed with tenacious old trees. Directly below the mountain and 5 miles (8 km) from the trailhead, you'll pass your last reliable water source, an icy cold stream fed by snowmelt.

The route steepens as you make your final climb to the summit. To the west, views of the wild and remote Gladstone country unfold. Six

Old Glory Lookout

miles from the starting point you reach the lookout and the 7844-foot summit of Old Glory. The Valhalla Peaks pierce the northern sky. To the east lie prominent landmarks—the Columbia River, the trail smelter, and Abercrombie and Hooknose peaks. To the northwest, Nancy Greene Lake twinkles below. The old shelter is littered with graffiti but it'll do in an emergency. Watch where your dog walks because there is sharp debris strewn around.

Spend as much time on the summit as you'd like, then retrace your route back to the trail junction on Unnecessary Ridge. Descend via the Plewman Trail, which will deliver the two of you to your vehicle in 3 miles (5 km). It's a quick descent through a small basin that harbors snow into midsummer, then a retreat into mature forest with plenty of creeks. Two miles from the ridge and 10 miles from your start you'll cross Hanna Creek on a good bridge. Surrounded by giant cedars, Hanna makes for a nice place to soak tired and sore paws. Hike the final but easy mile back to the trailhead, and revel in your *new* Glory.

14. Champion Lakes

Location: Kootenay Country
Round Trip: 4 miles (6.5 km)
Hiking Time: 2 hours
High Point: 3500 feet
Elevation Gain: Negligible
Maps: Champion Lakes Provincial Park, 82 F/4 Rossland-Trail
Best Hiking Time: May through October
Contact: BC Parks, Kootenay Division, (250) 489-8540
Note: Dogs need to be leashed and are not allowed on the beach.

Driving Directions: From Trail, British Columbia, drive east on BC 3B for 13 miles (21 km) through Montrose and Fruitvale to a junction with Champion Lakes Road (sign at junction). Turn left and follow this paved road 6 miles (10 km) to Champion Lakes Provincial Park. Bear right at the first junction (left goes to day-use beach) and continue 1.5 miles

Loop trip to First Champion Lake

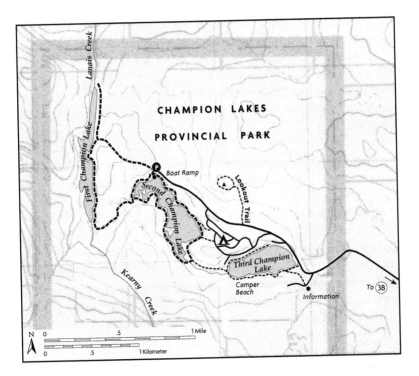

CHAMPION LAKES

PROVINCIAL PARK

Lanais Creek

First Champion Lake

Boat Ramp

Second Champion Lake

Lookout Trail

Third Champion Lake

Camper Beach

Information

Kearny Creek

To 3B

N 0 .5 1 Mile

0 .5 1 Kilometer

(2.5 km), passing the campground to the road's end and a trailhead signed "1st Lake Trail and Canoe Portage."

When the Columbia River valley begins to swelter in the summer sun, hordes of relief seekers from nearby Trail and Castlegar head to the 3000-acre Champion Lakes Provincial Park. Can you blame them? At an elevation of 2000 feet above the valley, a cool forest of pine and fir envelop three pretty and peaceful lakes. Most visitors come here to swim or fish; a few canoe and a few stay the night in the ninety-five-site campground; only a handful take to the trails, which means that you and your dog will have plenty of room to roam.

Since most activity occurs at the third lake, the other two lakes are a better choice for you and your furry friend to explore. A nice 4-mile loop can be made around these two lakes, but if you want to walk more, side trails can be added.

Begin by hiking the trail that branches right, signed "1st Lake." You'll be returning on the trail to your left, signed "2nd Lake Loop." Immediately enter a mature forest of larch, aspen, and Douglas fir. The landscape is boggy. If you come here early in the summer you'll be greeted by millions of mosquitoes. Fall is nicer—no bugs and a golden canopy.

After 0.75 mile of easy walking on a slight descent you'll come to the shore of the first lake and a trail junction signed "2nd Lake Parking and Boat Launch." The trail on your right goes 0.5 mile to the outlet of the first lake. It's a nice walk under big larches and along grassy shores. Watch for moose.

To continue the loop, head left, continuing along the first lake. It's a wonderfully flat hike along marshy shores. Lots of grassy islands dot the sliver lake, and birds are abundant. Half a mile from the junction you'll come to the lake's inlet. Now follow the stream 0.5 mile up to the second lake and another junction. The trail on the left goes a mile back to the parking lot, giving you the option of a shorter loop. The longer loop and preferred hike goes right. The second lake is bigger and deeper than the first, with lots of coves. Your dog's ears will perk at all the loon cries. Continue around the lake, avoiding all side trails on your right—they lead to the third lake or the campground. After 2 miles of very pleasant hiking around the second lake you'll return to the parking lot.

If you want to see what all of these lakes look like from above, hike

Champion Lake before sunset

the 1-mile Lookout Trail to a series of open ledges. The trail is dry, so bring water. It begins about a mile from the Loop Trail parking lot.

15. Panther Lake

Location: Kootenay Country
Round Trip: 5 miles (8 km)
Hiking Time: 3 hours
High Point: 5750 feet
Elevation Gain: 1750 feet
Map: 82 F/3 Salmo
Best Hiking Time: late June through October
Contact: British Columbia Ministry of Forests, Arrow Lake and
    Boundary District, Castlegar Ranger Station, (250) 365-8600

Driving Directions: From Castlegar, British Columbia, head west on BC 3 to the junction of BC 6 in Salmo. Turn right (south) and follow BC 3/6 for 4.5 miles, turning left onto Airport Road (look for sign for Salmo Golf Course; if coming from the south the turnoff is approximately 10.5 miles from the border crossing in Nelway). Follow this paved road for 0.75 mile. Just after crossing Sheep Creek and past an old lumber yard make a sharp right onto Sheep Creek Road. Follow this road east. In 1.5 miles bear right at a fork. Pass a campground in 6.5 miles. In 7.25 miles bear right and pass mining ruins. One mile beyond the ruins come to a junction (8.5 miles from Airport Road). Park here in a grassy spot off of the road. The road to the right goes to the Curtis Lake Trail; the left road (signed "Panther Road") goes to the trailhead for Panther Lake.

There are over two dozen alpine lakes scattered about in the high cirques and valleys of the Nelson Range. Some are quite difficult to get to, others have had logging roads punched right to their shores. On the west slope of Three Sisters Peak lie three aquatic gems: Waldie, Curtis,

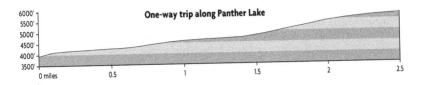

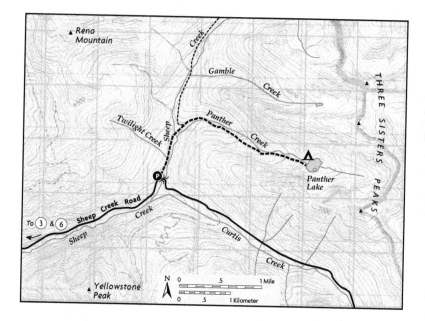

and Panther. Panther is the easiest to get to and a good choice for an afternoon hike with your best friend.

Although the actual trail to Panther is only 1.25 miles (2 km), most hikers who care about their vehicles will want to start their hike an additional 1.25 miles from the trailhead, beginning from where the road splits (the suggested parking spot). The road walk doubles the distance to 2.5 miles, still short enough for a quick escape.

Begin by walking the steep and rocky Panther Road. In 0.5 mile you'll cross roaring Sheep Creek on a bridge. Ten minutes beyond you'll come to a fork. Go right, and in 10 minutes you'll come to the official trailhead. The trail begins at the edge of an old clear-cut. Watch for bear sign—both grizzly and black live in these hills.

Enter a wet area of dense undergrowth. Make noise to give bears a heads-up. Soon you'll cross Panther Creek and enter a beautiful old-growth hemlock forest. The trail, an old mining route, is steep in places but well maintained.

As you ascend up the vertical slope, you never drift far from Panther Creek. Its roar accompanies you all the way to the lake. After 1 mile of climbing you come to Panther Lake, tucked in tightly under Three Sisters Peak. Bear grass and huckleberries line the shores. There are lots of big boulders for lounging or jumping into the water. Snow remains in the basin

Bear tracks along the trail to Panther Lake

late, so your dog may be going in without you. There are a couple of good camping spots by the outlet, and the high country beyond makes for some good exploring. Of course there's nothing wrong with just sitting on one of the warm rocks and gazing out at the twinkling waters all afternoon.

16. Wilson Creek

Location: Kootenay Country
Round Trip: 7.5 miles (12 km)
Hiking Time: 4 hours
High Point: 3000 feet
Elevation Gain: 400 feet
Map: 82 K/3
Best Hiking Time: June through October
Contact: BC Parks, Kootenay Division, (250) 489-8540

Driving Directions: From the historic and scenic village of New Denver, British Columbia, travel north on BC 6 for 3.5 miles. Just before

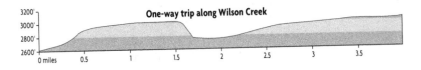

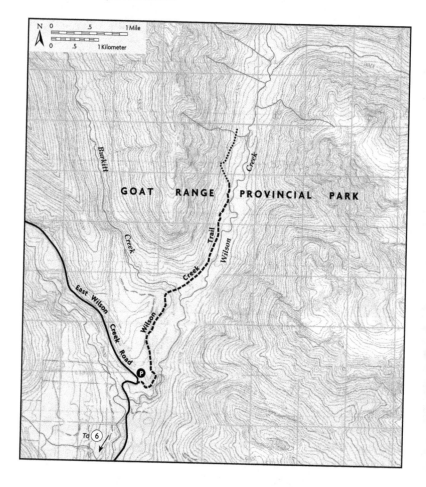

approaching Roseberry Provincial Park, turn right (east) onto East Wilson Creek Road. The turnoff is just before the bridge over Wilson Creek. Proceed on East Wilson Creek Road, which soon becomes the Wilson Creek Forest Road. Follow this gravel road for 7.5 miles (12 km) to the Wilson Creek Trailhead, located 0.5 mile after the bridge that crosses Wilson Creek. Park on the left side of the road about 100 feet north of the trailhead.

Here's an opportunity to hike in a wilderness park up a seldom-visited valley. Wilson Creek is located in BC's Goat Range Provincial Park, an area consisting of over 200,000 acres of some of the wildest country in the West Kootenay. Tucked between Valhalla Provincial Park and Purcell

Wilderness Conservancy Park, Goat Range Park may not be as well known as these neighboring sanctuaries, but it is just as beautiful and ecologically important. Furthermore, Goat Range Park—unlike Valhalla and nearby Kokanee Glacier Provincial Park—doesn't prohibit your four-legged friend from visiting.

But before your buddy gets his tail wagging out of control you might be thinking "Isn't this grizzly country?" It is, but the Wilson Creek Trail stays out of prime griz habitat, shunning those coveted alpine meadows to run along a roaring waterway fed by surrounding glaciers. The highlights of this hike include a primeval cedar forest and divine solitude.

While the chance for running into a grizzly is low, there's always the possibility. Keep your buddy nearby and be alert. There are plenty of black bear, moose, and cougar in the valley, too. And there is one other major concern to consider before setting off on this hike: lack of trail maintenance. Goat Provincial Range Park is a new park, carved from crown forest land. BC Parks now administers this tract, but due to provincial government budget woes does not have the funds or personnel to manage it. Since becoming a park in the mid-1990s there has been virtually no trail maintenance. The Wilson Creek Trail is in fair shape, but expect some brushy areas and one possible problem area, the crossing of Burkitt Creek. The bridge over Burkitt Creek washed out several years ago and has not been replaced. The crossing must now be done over a logjam, which is safe for most sure-footed dogs and their owners. However, expect this jam to shift over the years, and be prepared to turn around if the crossing appears too difficult. A quick hike out and a trip to the nearby and well-maintained lower Wilson Creek Trail (accessed from a forest road that leaves from Rosebery Provincial Park) will still allow you to enjoy this wild country.

The hike begins on an old road that maps show as drivable; however, encroaching willows and alders make driving extremely difficult. With the roar of Wilson Falls in the distance, walk this pleasant forest road 1.5 miles to the actual trailhead marked by a trail post. The route is fairly obvious, but at about 0.3 mile watch for an unsigned junction. Stay left.

From the trailhead the trail drops down to river and works its way across an outwash area. Two miles from your start you'll come to Burkitt Creek. If you and your intrepid four-legged friend can safely cross it, you'll have an old-growth forest all to yourselves. From here the trail traverses a hemlock grove before climbing a bank above the roaring river. Through

Old-growth western red cedar along the Wilson Creek Trail

a dark tunnel of stunted cedars the trail works its way up valley. The clear path through the surrounding vegetation doubles as a wildlife corridor. Your dog will have a field day sniffing out all of the wildlife signs.

The trail eventually drops back down to river and enters an impressive old-growth cedar forest. Three miles from your start you'll come to the ruins of an old shelter. Here you can access the river on a nice gravel bar. Continue up the valley to bigger and older trees. At 3.5 miles an exceptional cedar towers above, followed by yet more amazing ancient trees. On a hot day this hike offers the closest thing to an air-conditioned trail—the old-growth forest traps the cool air coming off Wilson Creek.

At 3.75 miles the trail makes a sharp turn left and climbs away from the forest floor. This is a good spot to turn around—beyond this point the trail rapidly deteriorates and soon becomes impassable. Admire all of those trees again on your return and enjoy this wild valley in the heart of the Kootenay.

17. Pilot Bay

Location: Kootenay Country
Round Trip: 4 miles (6.5 km)
Hiking Time: 2 hours
High Point: 2000 feet
Elevation Gain: 200 feet
Map: 82 F/10 Crawford Bay
Best Hiking Time: late March to November
Contact: BC Parks, Kootenay Division, (250) 489-8540
Note: Dogs must be leashed.

Driving Directions: From the junction of BC 3 and BC 3A in Creston, British Columbia, drive north on BC 3A. Follow this beautiful highway along the east shore of Kootenay Lake 48 miles (78 km) to the Kootenay Bay ferry landing. (Alternatively, you can arrive here from Nelson by traveling 21 miles (34 km) east on BC 3A to the Balfour ferry landing.) Just before approaching the ferry queue turn left (south) onto Pilot Bay Road. Follow this road for 2 miles to a junction signed "Pilot Bay Provincial Park, Marine Park/Trails." Turn left. In 500 feet you'll come

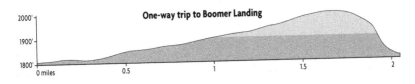

One-way trip to Boomer Landing

to the trailhead and a small parking lot. Be sure not to block the gate that leads to an adjacent private residence.

Pilot Bay Provincial Park offers a great leg stretcher early in the season when the surrounding peaks are buried in snow, late in the season when they're buried again, and during the hot summer months when a hike to a refreshing and secluded beach is in order. Offering the best trail

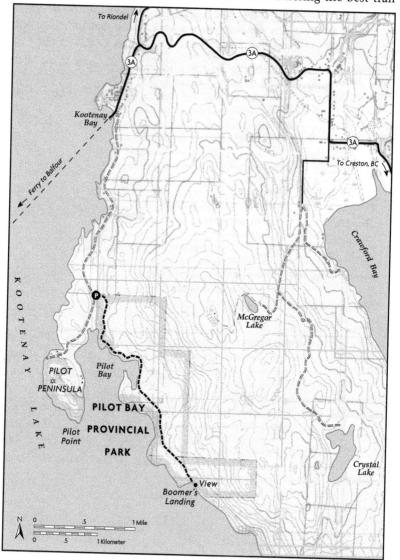

Mittens at Kootenay Lake, Boomer's Landing in Pilot Bay Provincial Park

system along the shores of massive Kootenay Lake, this 850-acre park protects almost 3 miles of scenic shoreline on the Pilot Peninsula. (**Note:** Pilot is the common name of the peninsula—the actual name is Crawford, which is also the name of the fingerlike bay on the east side of this protruding land mass.)

Pilot Bay Provincial Park is loved by the locals. Its trails are well maintained, and although the park gets plenty of visitors (a good number arrive by boat), even on the hottest days there's still plenty of room at Pilot Bay's scenic beaches. The hike to Boomer's Landing offers the prettiest beach in the park.

As the name indicates, Boomer's Landing was once a log boom—a point of contact for cut timber to be tugged across Kootenay Lake to mills. In fact much of the present park was the site of past logging and milling. Walking among the park's tall pines and cedars—and looking out upon a shoreline that appears to be pristine—it's now hard to imagine that such a beautiful place was once hopping with industry. Pilot Bay offers sound evidence of nature's resilience.

None of this, of course, matters to your dog! This is just a great place to go for a hike and an even better place for a swim. The hike to Boomer's Landing is nearly level, a 2-mile trot that can be undertaken by just about any canine. The shady trail is wide and soft. Be aware of poison oak, and don't go sniffing off the trail.

The trail begins in cool forest and commences in a series of ups and downs as it rounds a ledge above the lake. Here, along a warm southern exposure, junipers and ponderosa pines thrive. In about 0.75 mile a spur turns to Sawmill Bay, once the site of a sawmill. The beach isn't too appealing, but walking along the soft, cushiony shoreline (composed of compressed sawdust) has a certain novelty. If your dog isn't intrigued by the spongy beach, the numerous waterfowl in the bay will keep her captivated, as Mittens was by the geese and mergansers.

Beyond Sawmill Bay the trail continues through a cool cedar forest and along a shallow mosquito-infested cove. Soon a trail branches right to a small peninsula housing a developed hike-in or boat-in campground. Continue straight, passing another spur trail, this one leading to a good beach.

In another mile you'll come to a signed trail junction. Go right to Boomer's Landing. After passing the remains of a few cabins, the two of you will soon emerge on a wide, cobbled beach. Before plunging into the refreshing waters of Kootenay Lake, enjoy the view. With steep towering mountains on both sides of the fjordlike lake, you may feel like you're on Howe Sound, though these waters are a heck of a lot warmer. Just ask Buddy, a black Lab from Kimberly, BC. This is his favorite beach in the Kootenay region. He doesn't mind sharing Boomer's Landing with you and your pup. Just be sure to play fetch with him—in the water, of course.

18. Lockhart Creek

Location: Kootenay Country
Round Trip: 9 miles (14 km)
Hiking Time: 4–5 hours
High Point: 4400 feet
Elevation Gain: 2600 feet
Maps: 82 F/10 Crawford Bay, 82 F/7 Boswell
Best Hiking Time: May to November
Contact: BC Parks, Kootenay Division, (250) 489-8540

Driving Directions: From the junction of BC 3 and BC 3A in Creston, British Columbia, drive north on BC 3A along the east shore of Kootenay Lake 32 miles (52 km) to Lockhart Beach Provincial Park. Park in the small day-use parking lot on the east side of the highway. Walk up the paved path through the picnic area to the campground. The trail begins near campsite 18. Your dog must be on a leash while in the campground and day-use area.

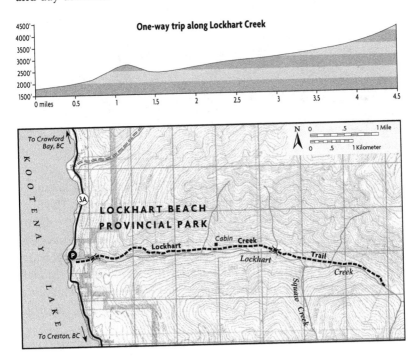

Lockhart Creek

One of the last intact watersheds along the eastern shore of Kootenay Lake, Lockhart Creek has been protected as a provincial park. The tumbling creek dissects this 9200-acre (3734 hectares) green swath, and its accompanying trail is your only portal into this wilderness. Traveling through the heart of the park, the Lockhart Creek Trail is a sheer delight for both human and hound, hugging the cascading creek through cool, damp forest for most of the way. This hike is a good choice on hot and rainy days, for the thick forest canopy keeps you sheltered from both sun and rain.

Start the hike by traveling through the picnic area to the campground.

A sign near site 18 marks the beginning. The well-defined path skirts the campground, crosses an adjacent private campground, and quickly emerges on Lockhart Road. Turn left and walk 100 meters on this road to a sign pointing out the trail to your left. On a good bridge cross the creek and enter Lockhart Creek Provincial Park. Civilization will now be left behind.

Immediately come to a junction. Head right (the left leads back to BC 3A, an alternative start). The trail follows the creek—sometimes closely, at other times on a bluff high above it—through a narrow valley. Occasional breaks in the vegetation allow for glimpses of steep and towering peaks and ridges.

Utilizing old roads and paths, the trail is well-constructed and well-maintained (thanks to the Lockhart Creek Heritage Committee). The first 0.5 mile travels along the rocky waterway, where elk and deer have created paths to the creek.

Moving upcreek the trail makes a steep climb to avoid a very narrow bottom passage, then drops back down to water level. A big cedar at 1.25 miles provides a great spot to contemplate the creek's beauty. The trail continues up the valley, undulating between cool cedar groves and drier pockets of birch.

You'll occasionally notice old mile markers. These signs are holding tough, for Canada has been on the metric system for over 30 years. In 2.5 miles you'll come to the remains of an old cabin. This is a good turnaround for a shorter hike. If your dog continues up the trail, the two of you will do a little climbing again above the creek. In 3 miles you'll cross a brushy avalanche chute—watch out for nettles. In 4 miles you'll meet up with Lockhart again, this time in a beautiful grove of old-growth hemlock. The trail works its way through the ancient forest and at 4.5 miles crosses the cascading creek on an old bridge. This is a good point for day hikers to turn around.

If you want to continue, use caution on the sketchy bridge. The trail continues for another 5 miles, climbing steeply into the Purcell Mountains, topping out at an elevation of 2134 meters (7000 ft.). From the alpine ridge it descends to Baker Lake.

You don't need to hike the entire trail to enjoy this wilderness park. The trip just along Lockhart Creek should leave both you and your dog quite content.

Note: Dogs are not allowed on Lockhart Beach; however, a handful of enjoyable beaches lie just south along BC 3A.

KETTLE RIVER MOUNTAIN RANGE

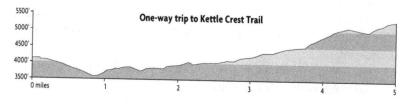

19. Big Lick

Location: Kettle River Mountains
Round Trip: 10 miles
Hiking Time: 5 hours
High Point: 5200 feet
Elevation Gain: 1200 feet
Map: USGS Mt. Leona
Best Hiking Time: May through October
Contact: Colville National Forest, Republic Ranger District, (509) 775-3305

Driving Directions: From Republic, Washington, take State Route 21 north to the small village of Malo. Continue 1.5 miles north of Malo, turning right (east) on the Aeneas Creek Road (County Road 566). In 3.75 miles enter the Colville National Forest where the road becomes Forest Road 2160. Proceed 1.75 miles more on this rougher road to a sign on the right stating, "Trail Access." Proceed right 0.25 mile on this narrow spur road to the trailhead, or park and walk.

One-way trip to Kettle Crest Trail

5500'
5000'
4500'
4000'
3500'
0 miles   1   2   3   4   5

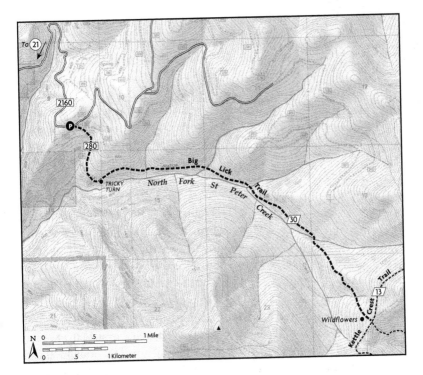

What hiking dog wouldn't be interested in a trail called Big Lick? But before you get your best buddy all worked up, this trail isn't lined with kibble or last night's leftovers. Neither are there legions of sweaty hikers to greet. What's to lick then? Just miles of Kettle Mountain wilderness morsels and your face, of course, upon completing a great day's hike.

The Big Lick offers some of the best wildlife habitat in the Kettles. Your dog's nose will be in high gear sniffing out all of the creatures that have scurried before him on this quiet trail. Bear, deer, moose, cougars, martens, grouse, and coyotes all have left behind plenty of tracks, scents, and scat. What's missing are the two-legged creatures. The Big Lick sees very few hikers.

This trail might have become a memory if the folks at the Kettle Range Conservation Group (KRCG) hadn't adopted it 15 years ago, then reopened and maintained it. Now it is a showcase, introducing hikers to a Kettle Mountain rarity—a large valley of old-growth forest. Much of the surrounding slopes have succumbed to either the ax or the flame. The Big Lick allows you and your dog to enjoy a cool and damp forest, another rarity in these parts.

The trail begins on an old forest road, descending gently on an open

Dusty pauses along Big Lick Trail.

southern slope graced with giant ponderosa pines and views of Mount Leona to St. Peters Creek at about 2 miles. Follow the gently flowing creek through a burned area, followed by a mature forest at about 2.5 miles, where giant larches survived the wildfires. Thimbleberries flourish here—a treat for you and the bears to lick.

The trail crosses the creek several times on bridges. Lack of water is never a concern on this hike. As the trail continues to make its very gentle climb to the Kettle Crest, the forest becomes older, damper, and cooler. The two of you may spot a barred owl here, not an uncommon sight. Stop and admire the handful of giant larches.

After 5 miles of some of the nicest and easiest hiking in all of the Kettles, Big Lick Trail 30 comes to an end at a four-way junction. Straight ahead the Ryan Cabin Trail descends to the South Fork of Boulder Creek. North and south, Kettle Crest Trail 13 runs the ridge and traverses many high peaks of the range. If you and your buddy aren't licked yet, venture along the Kettle Crest for a mile or two to views and more beautiful mature forest.

20. Mount Leona

Location: Kettle River Mountains
Round Trip: 7 miles
Hiking Time: 4 hours
High Point: 6474 feet
Elevation Gain: 1325 feet
Map: USGS Mt. Leona
Best Hiking Time: June through October
Contact: Colville National Forest, Republic Ranger District,
(509) 775-3305

Driving Directions: From Republic, Washington, take State Route 21 north to the small village of Malo. Turn right onto St. Peters Creek Road

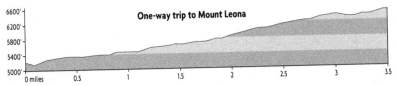

(County Road 584). In 1 mile the pavement ends. In 1.7 miles bear right. In 3 miles you enter the national forest, and in 5.6 miles you come to a fork and bear left onto Forest Road 2157. The trailhead is 9.5 miles from Malo at a large clearing on the left.

An easy climb, Mount Leona offers far-reaching views and a chance for you and your dog to explore some lonely country. That's the good news. The bad news is that ol' Leona has been through some tough times. Wildfires in 2001 scorched her summit, and earlier fires raised havoc on her eastern slopes. The burnt areas, if left alone, will do just fine over time; however, this is range country and wayward bovines haven't been allowing the mountain to recover.

Still, the views are wonderful and there are nice pockets of primeval forest along the way. Raptors catch thermals above while busy nuthatches work the woods. Your dog's ears will constantly be piqued as she tries to decipher the nonstop avian cacophony. City dogs may be intrigued by the "mooing deer" that linger at the trailhead. "Mittens, that's where hamburger comes from!"

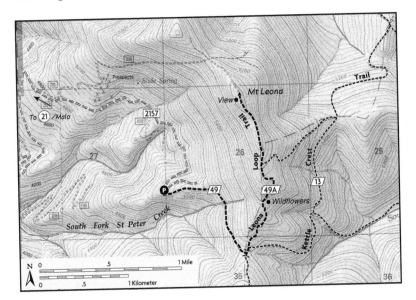

Heather and Mittens, Mount Leona Trail junction along Kettle Crest Trail

Be sure your dog is well controlled on this trail, for there are several herds of future hamburger in the area. The trail begins in a large open area on an old road. Leona's open southern slopes rise above as you skirt east around the mountain. In about 10 minutes you'll come to a small clearing with a view. To the west the golden, rolling hills of the Curlew Creek valley roll out before you.

About 15 minutes from the trailhead you'll leave the old road and head left on a short, steep section of trail. The grade soon lessens onto a side slope through old-growth fir. You'll come to a spring and stock trough at 1.2 miles. Water sources beyond are less reliable. At 1.6 miles Leona Trail 49 comes to a signed junction at a saddle on the Kettle Crest (5550 ft.). The trail straight ahead and on your right is Kettle Crest Trail 13, leading to points north and south along the ridge. For Mount Leona take the trail to your left, the Leona Loop Trail 49A.

This is a nice trail through mature timber, grassy openings, and small ledges. Work your way up Leona's southeast shoulder. The loop trail breaks out into open meadows after about 1.5 miles. Here the trail turns north, skirts around the mountain, and descends back to the Kettle Crest Trail. This section of trail is very hard to follow, overgrown and buried in windfall. It is not recommended. No concern though, for the two of you are going to head straight up the open slopes to the 6474-foot summit of Mount Leona. In about 0.5 mile you'll come to the summit, nearly burnt to a crisp except for the weather tower. Concentrate instead on the view. The verdant slopes of Copper Butte, Profanity Peak, and Taylor Ridge add a nice contrast to the charcoal summit of Leona. Make sure your dog isn't taking an ash bath in a charred wallow.

21. Copper Butte

Location: Kettle River Mountains
Round Trip: 9.5 miles
Hiking Time: 6 hours
High Point: 7140 feet
Elevation Gain: 2390 feet
Map: USGS Copper Butte
Best Hiking Time: late May through October
Contact: Colville National Forest, Republic Ranger District,
(509) 775-3305

Driving Directions: From Republic, Washington, head east on State Route 20. Turn north on SR 21 and follow it for just under 3 miles to a four-way junction. Turn right (east) on gravel County Road 284 (Fish Hatchery Road). Just shy of 3 miles bear left at a major junction. At Echo Bay Mine bear right on the less obvious Forest Road 2152. Follow this narrow road for 3 miles to FR 2040. Bear left onto FR 2040 for 5 miles to the junction with FR 250 where a sign for Marcus Trail 8 points right. In 1.5 miles, come to a small clearing, a former log yard, on your left. This is the trailhead, marked by a small sign at 4750 feet.

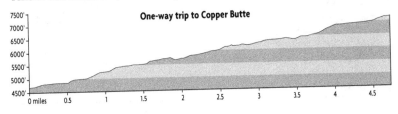

Copper Butte is the highest summit in the Kettle River Mountains, Washington's forgotten range. There are several ways to reach this lofty eastern Washington peak, but none as beautiful as the Marcus Trail. Once part of a route that extended to the small town of Marcus on the confluence of the Kettle and Columbia Rivers, now only 3.5 miles of the trail remain. Use is light and mainly by four-legged travelers—equestrians, cattle, and the occasional coyote.

The Marcus Trail should provide you and your pup with a lonely trek into the heart of the Kettles. The view alone from Copper Butte is worth the journey. The entire Kettle Range can be observed from the old lookout site. BC's Rossland Range, Idaho's Selkirks and western Washington's Cascades can all be seen from this prominent peak. But it is the miles of alpine meadows on the way to the summit that really make this a supreme hike, one of my all-time favorites in the entire Inland Northwest.

Despite its remoteness, this trail is fairly well maintained. Water is plentiful along the first 2.5 miles through streams and troughs. But it can get pretty hot in the Kettles, so be sure to carry plenty of water. A handful of bovines range the lower meadows, so unless your dog is an accustomed range rover, be sure your Rover raises no beef and stays by your side.

The trail begins in an open forest of giant ponderosa pine and Douglas fir. In 0.5 mile you'll enter a large area that burned in the early 1990s. A mini forest of lodgepole pines is slowly gaining on the blackened and silver snags. Plenty of fireweed adds a purple hue to the understory. You'll soon reenter a mature forest of fir and larch. In 2 miles the trees begin to yield to hundreds of acres of resplendent meadows. Snow melts early on

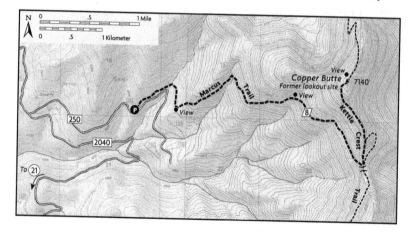

Fireweed thrives in burn areas near Copper Butte.

these south-facing slopes, so the flowers begin to bloom by May. There'll be a variety for you to view and your dog to chew.

In 2.5 miles you'll come to a spring and trough, the last reliable water on this hike. The trail continues through glorious meadows. The views are good, but the floral show is even better.

After 3.5 miles you'll reenter the forest and come to an intersection with Kettle Crest Trail 13 in a high saddle along the ridge (6400 ft.). Turn left and head north 1.25 easy miles through open forest and meadows to the summit of Copper Butte (7140 ft.), where a lookout tower once stood. Not much of it remains, but be careful of rusted nails and broken glass. Roam the nearby meadows instead.

22. Wapaloosie Mountain

Location: Kettle River Mountains
Round Trip: 6 miles
Hiking Time: 5 hours
High Point: 7018 feet
Elevation Gain: 2000 feet
Map: USGS Copper Butte
Best Hiking Time: May through October
Contact: Colville National Forest, Three Rivers Ranger District, Kettle Falls, (509) 775-3305

Driving Directions: From Republic, Washington, head east on State Route 20 for 21 miles, and turn left (north) onto Forest Road 2030 (Albion Hill Road). From Kettle Falls, Washington, head west on SR 20 for 22 miles, and turn right onto FR Road 2030. The road is located 4 miles east of Sherman Pass. Follow FR 2030, a winding gravel road for 3.3 miles to the trailhead, located on your left at 5000 feet. The trailhead is signed and begins in a small campground.

One of the highest summits on the Kettle Crest, Wapaloosie Mountain offers extensive views and some of the finest alpine meadows in eastern Washington. With a predominantly southeastern exposure, the Wapaloosie Trail melts outs early, allowing you and your dog some great early-season high-country hiking. However, this blessing can be a curse, because after late June water can be scarce on this peak. Pack extra for you and Lassie.

Although Wapaloosie's lofty reaches often bake in the sun, the foot of this mountain is surrounded by extensive wetlands. There's always a chance to spot a wayward moose, but you're guaranteed to come within striking distance of a much more prolific critter: the dreaded mosquito! In early summer they breed, swarm, and launch a mean offensive at the trailhead.

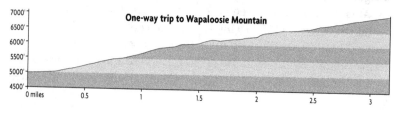

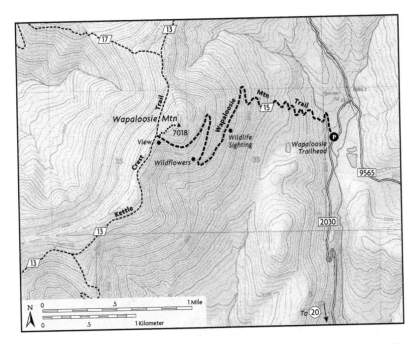

Wapaloosie Mountain Trail 15 is well maintained, thanks to the Kettle Mountain Backcountry Horsemen. The trail begins in a thick forest of lodgepole pine. Within a few minutes you'll cross a tributary of the North Fork of Sherman Creek. This is the only reliable water source on this hike. The trail starts out easy and then gets down to business.

In 1 mile (6000 ft.) you'll break out from the forest and begin traversing the majestic meadows of Wapaloosie. The going gets easier as the trail ascends through a series of long switchbacks. The eastern side of the Kettles sees little range activity, and native fescue grasses proliferate here. Wildflowers brush pastels and bright colors across the meadows. Sun-baked sage permeates the air.

Views range from BC's Rossland Range to the Abercrombie-Hooknose highlands. The Twin Sisters, Mack Mountain and King Mountain, stand out like emerald sentinels guarding the eastern flank of the Kettle Crest. Of course your dog won't be interested in this—he'll be excited by all the meadow madness around him: flickering birds in the sage, scurrying ground squirrels in the grasses, and flitting butterflies in the blossoms.

In 2.7 miles you'll reach the Kettle Crest Trail 13 (6850 ft.). From this junction it's a short and easy off-trail ramble to Wapaloosie's 7018-foot

Mittens admires the view from Wapaloosie Mountain Trail.

summit. Head northeast through meadows and open forest of Engelmann spruce and white-bark pine. It'll take about 10 minutes to reach the broad summit of the mountain.

23. Snow Peak Cabin

Location: Kettle River Mountains
Round Trip: 6.4 miles
Hiking Time: 4 hours
High Point: 6320 feet
Elevation Gain: 1500 feet
Map: USGS Sherman Peak
Best Hiking Time: June through October
Contact: Colville National Forest, Republic Ranger District,
(509) 775-3305

Driving Directions: From Republic, Washington, head east on State Route 20 for 7 miles. Just beyond milepost 309 turn right onto Hall Creek Road (Forest Road 99). Follow this good gravel road for 3.25 miles, turning left just beyond a cattle guard onto Snow Peak Road (FR 2059-100). In 4.75 miles, high above the valley, find the trailhead on your right.

This is one of my favorite hikes in the Kettles. It's short and sweet, instantly putting you into the high country. This entire hike is within the White Mountain burn of 1988, so shade doesn't exist. However, there are only 1500 feet of climbing and it is almost always windy along this trail. You'll be mystified by the ghostly silver snags that line the way. Fireweed and aster paint the regenerating forest floor. Your dog will be captivated by the number of ground squirrels that have colonized the burnt zone.

From the trailhead, waste no time in climbing. A few surviving trees provide some greenery. The trail is grassy here (planted after the fire to prevent erosion) so watch for ticks early in the season. After 2 miles of good trail you'll come to a high point on the ridge, with good views south to Edds and Bald mountains. You'll notice the Snow Peak cabin, too, just below Bald.

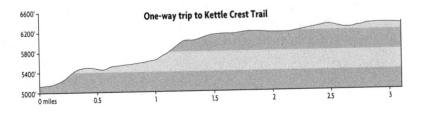

One-way trip to Kettle Crest Trail

Snow Peak Trail wildflowers in the 1988 White Mountain burn region

Now begin a short descent. Lofty Snow Peak looms above and in front of you. In 2.7 miles reach the junction with the Kettle Crest Trail 13. Turn right (south). From here the cabin is an easy 0.5-mile hike. Enjoy extensive views west through the silver and black forest.

The cabin lies just off of the main trail—watch for a sign. A reliable spring is nearby. Although built by the Forest Service as a winter shelter for cross-county skiers, hikers are invited to stay overnight, too. It's a nice

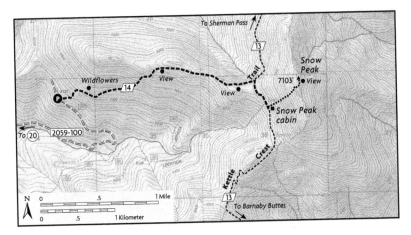

facility, with space for about eight people (or six people and two dogs!). On summer weekends it's likely that others will be there; during the week the place will probably be all yours.

The summit of 7103-foot Snow Peak makes for a good cross-country ramble. Although steep, it's all meadows. The view from the summit is amazing, from the Rossland Range to Lake Roosevelt. If it's early summer, there might even be some snow along the way.

24. Barnaby Buttes

Location: Kettle River Mountains
Round Trip: 5.5 miles
Hiking Time: 4 hours
High Point: 6534 feet
Elevation Gain: 2000 feet
Map: USGS Sherman Peak
Best Hiking Time: June through October
Contact: Colville National Forest, Three Rivers Ranger District, (509) 775-3305

Driving Directions: From Republic, Washington, travel east on State Route 20 to Sherman Pass. At milepost 323, 3.5 miles east of the pass, make a sharp right on gravel Forest Road 2020, signed "South Fork Sherman Creek." Follow FR 2020 for 7 miles to FR 2014, signed "Barnaby Creek" (From Kettle Falls travel west on SR 20, turning left on FR 2020

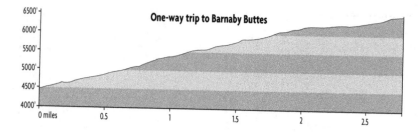

just after milepost 332). Continue on FR 2014 for 0.25 mile. Immediately after a creek crossing turn right onto FR 500. A big sign for Barnaby Buttes and the Kettle Crest indicates the way. In 1 mile bear left at a fork. It's drivable but overgrown. Park here and walk 1.5 miles to the trailhead, or sacrifice your vehicle's paint job.

This is a straightforward hike to one of the loneliest summits on the Kettle Crest. It also offers one of the easiest approaches to the lofty Kettle high country. The Barnaby Buttes Trail utilizes an old fire tower service road, which is now a wide, gentle trail.

The trail begins by a tumbling little creek (4500 ft.) and traverses a lush forest of pine and larch. Ample shade along the way will keep you and your pooch from overheating. Your buddy will probably pick up the scents of resident bruins: bear scat, tracks, and scratches are abundant

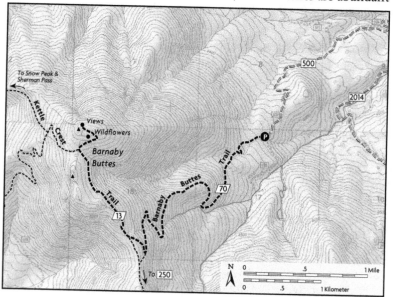

along this trail. Keep your intrepid pup close.

In 0.4 mile you'll come to a refreshing creek and a reliable water source. Through old cuts and old growth the trail leads higher onto the Kettle Crest. Lupine line the way as the trail meanders through groves of mature timber. In late summer, stop to munch on ripe huckleberries; in fall, admire golden larches. In 1.4 miles you'll come to a stream crossing, reliable in all but the driest summers. Shortly afterwards the trail enters a large burned area, where a lush new forest is slowly moving in on the silver and blackened snags. The views are good: To the south, White Mountain's "white" slopes of talus and granite shimmer in the afternoon sun; to the east, the emerald peaks and valleys of the South Fork Sherman Creek fan out below. A couple of long switchbacks bring you to the Kettle Crest.

Coyote along the Barnaby Buttes Trail

After 1.75 miles the Barnaby Buttes Trail comes to a junction with the Kettle Crest Trail 13 (6050 ft.). The left-hand trail (south) climbs to the summit of White Mountain, the right-hand (north) goes to the Buttes. For 0.75 mile Trail 13 works its way up to a broad gap (6350 ft.) between the two buttes. An easy-to-miss sign perched on a big snag points out the way to the old lookout site on the north butte. The trail has all but disappeared. No worries—the grassy and open forest summit is easy to negotiate. Aim for the high point (6534 ft.), about a 0.25-mile walk from the gap. The north butte is a lonely but beautiful place. Winds whistle through the snags and tall timber. Grasses sway. Deer, moose, bear, and coyote roam the slopes. The spirits from White Mountain can be heard in the evening breeze. Find the foundation of the old lookout, complete with stairway—the stairway to Kettle Mountain heaven.

25. Kettle Crest South

Location: Kettle River Mountain Range
One Way: 13.5 miles
Hiking Time: 2 days
High Point: 6923 feet
Elevation Gain: 3700 feet
Elevation Loss: 3200 feet
Map: USGS Sherman Peak
Best Hiking Time: June through October
Contact: Colville National Forest, Three Rivers Ranger District,
(509) 775-3305
Note: NW Forest pass required at Sherman Pass.

Driving Directions: From Republic, Washington, travel 17 miles east
on State Route 20 to Sherman Pass. The turnoff for the trailhead is on
the left (north) just past the pass. The large parking area with restrooms
is the northern terminus for the hike. To begin the hike proceed past
Sherman Pass, continuing east on SR 20. At milepost 323, 3.5 miles east
of the pass, make a sharp right on gravel Forest Road 2020, signed "South
Fork Sherman Creek." Follow it for 7 miles to FR 2014, signed "Barnaby
Creek." (From Kettle Falls travel west on SR 20, turning left on FR 2020
just after milepost 332.) Continue on FR 2014 for 4 miles. Turn right
onto FR 250 and proceed 4.25 miles. The trailhead will be on your right,
marked by a big sign and plenty of parking.

A national recreation trail, Kettle Crest Trail 13 traverses the spine of the
high Kettles from just south of White Mountain all the way to the Deer
Creek summit. It's a 42-mile journey, and except for the Sherman Pass
area you can pretty much expect to have this trail all to yourself and your
dog. One of Washington's finest high-country long-distance trails, it can
be hiked piecemeal when combined with spur trails, or all the way
through on a three- or four-night journey.

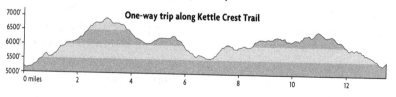

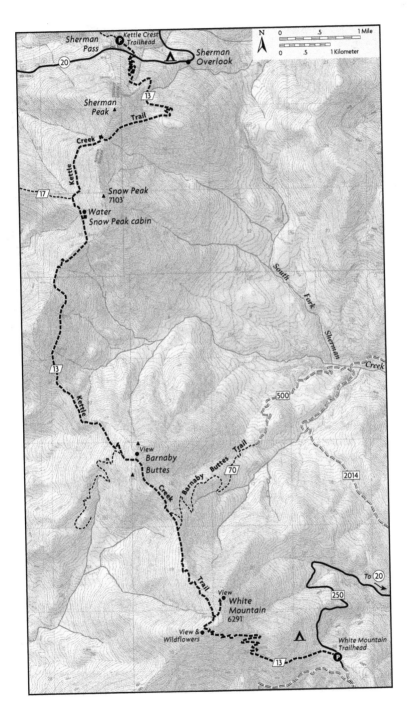

Sherman Pass
Sherman Peak ▲
Kettle Crest Trailhead
Sherman Overlook
13
Creek
Trail
20
17
Snow Peak 7103'
Water
Snow Peak cabin
Kettle
13
Kettle
South Fork Sherman
Creek
500
View
Barnaby Buttes
Barnaby Buttes Trail
70
2014
Creek
Trail
To 20
250
View
White Mountain 6291'
View & Wildflowers
White Mountain Trailhead
13
13

N

| 0 | | .5 | | 1 Mile |
| 0 | | .5 | | 1 Kilometer |

Craig Romano and Heather Scott hike the hot south slope of White Mountain.

The southern 13.5-mile section contains some of the range's most dramatic scenery and it can be done as a long day hike or an easy 2-day backpack. If a shuttle can be arranged I suggest traveling from south to north, getting the exposed White Mountain climb done early in the morning. The White Mountain fire of 1988 scorched much of the forest of the southern Kettles, and although the forest is rapidly regenerating you'd be wise to avoid this hike during hot, dry periods. While there is no shortage of panoramic views and sprawling tracts of gorgeous wildflowers, water is at a premium on this hike. It is best to go early in the summer when lingering snows provide runoff. Otherwise, it is absolutely imperative that you bring sufficient water for you and your buddy. Properly prepared and well-hydrated, the two of you can enjoy one of the most scenic hikes in eastern Washington. Wildlife are also prolific, especially bear and deer.

The trail begins by climbing the south slope of White Mountain via a series of wide switchbacks bordered by burnt snags and pockets of green. Be sure to let your pup rest in the scattered shaded spots while pushing for the summit.

In 3 miles find the fading spur trail leading right to White's 6291-foot summit. It's a 10-minute walk to the old lookout site. The views south to

Lake Roosevelt, west to the Cascades, east to the Selkirks, and north all along the Kettle Crest are impressive. White Mountain is a sacred peak to the Colville Confederated Tribes. Please make sure that you and your dog respect all artifacts on the summit, and do not disturb any of the cairns.

Just beyond the spur is a spring (may be dry by August). Through beautiful silver forests the Kettle Crest Trail now begins its long but gradual descent off White. In 5 miles you come to an intersection with the Barnaby Buttes Trail (Hike 24). Utilizing an old road, the trail works its way between the two buttes. Side trips to the summits are worthy objectives.

In 6 miles, just beyond where Trail 7 approaches from the west, there is a fairly reliable spring. Follow an up-and-down route to the saddle between the buttes and Bald Mountain, then begin a steep climb around Bald's eastern slopes. In 8 miles, there is another spring just before the junction with Trail 3.

After 9.5 miles of more ups and downs and great views, you'll arrive at the Snow Peak cabin (Hike 23), which has water nearby and is a great place to spend the night. Beyond the cabin the trail traverses meadows and ghost forests, working its way around lofty Snow Peak. In 10 miles, Trail 10 branches off west. Continue right on the Crest Trail, making one last climb to the saddle between Snow and Sherman Peaks at 11 miles. The Sherman Peak loop trail departs left—continue right, rounding Sherman, returning to a cool mature forest, and reaching the northern trailhead after 13.5 miles.

26. Emerald Lake

Location: Kettle River Mountain Range
Round Trip: 6.2 miles
Hiking Time: 3–4 hours
High Point: 3550 feet
Elevation Gain: 660 feet
Map: USGS Jackknife
Best Hiking Time: May to November
Contact: Colville National Forest, Three Rivers Ranger District, (509) 775-3305

Driving Directions: From Republic, Washington, travel east on State Route 20. Turn left on Forest Road 020 at milepost 337. (From Kettle

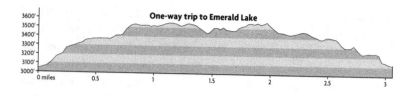

Falls travel west on SR 20. Turn right on FR 020 at milepost 337.) Follow FR 020 for 5 miles to its end at the Trout Lake Campground and Hoodoo Canyon Trailhead.

If you and your canine are itching for an early season adventure in Kettle Country, Emerald Lake should soothe that itch. Located in the heart of steep-walled, glacially carved Hoodoo Canyon, Emerald Lake is a little gem. The hike is short and easy, and you can easily spend all day in the canyon and along the shores of the secluded lake. The trail begins at pretty little Trout Lake at the head of the canyon. A little Forest Service campground with four secluded sites sits right on the lake and at the trailhead. Consider spending the night here. Don't forget your fishing gear.

Hoodoo Canyon Trail 17 starts off in a cool forest of cedar and fir. On

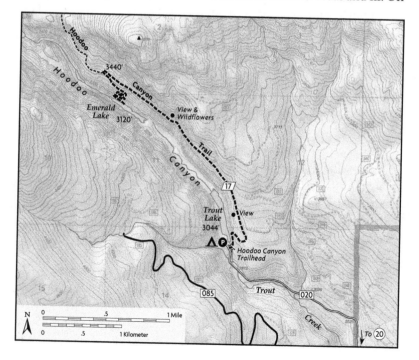

Pika on rocks near Emerald Lake

a good bridge cross the outlet of Trout Lake (3050 ft.) and immediately begin to climb. At first your surroundings are quite lush; the trail plows through a forest of salal, snowberry, current, thimbleberries, maple, birch, and your pal's favorite, dogwood. However, as you switchback out of the damp canyon to a ledge on the canyon wall, increased sun exposure means a drier and very different landscape. After about 0.4 mile the climb eases and you emerge high above Trout Lake.

Now the trail makes its way across a ledge on the eastern wall of the canyon. Giant ponderosa pines provide shade. It's safe going but keep your friend close because there are several exposed drops not too far from the trail. After 2 miles Emerald Lake comes into view far below in the canyon. A short descent begins across an open, grassy shelf, providing precious warmth in early season and brutal heat in July.

The junction with the Emerald Lake Trail 94 lies just beyond, at 3400 feet. The Hoodoo Canyon Trail continues right for 2 miles more, dropping 900 feet to Deadman Creek. Turn left on Trail 94 toward Emerald Lake. After dropping 200 feet on a 0.6-mile course the two of you will arrive at the shores of the lake (3120 ft.).

This is a great place to spend the day. Explore nearby boulder fields or take a nap by the water. In early season the lake is cold, and later in the year the lake is shallow. Your dog won't mind either way.

PEND OREILLE COUNTRY- SELKIRKS

27. Abercrombie Mountain

Location: Selkirk Mountains
Round Trip: 6.5 miles
Hiking Time: 4 hours
High Point: 7308 feet
Elevation Gain: 3220 feet
Map: USGS Abercrombie
Best Hiking Time: late June to mid-October
Contact: Colville National Forest, Colville Ranger District,
(509) 684-7000

Driving Directions: From the junction of US Highway 395 and State Route 20 in Colville, Washington, travel east on SR 20 for 1.1 miles. Across from the airport, turn left on Aladdin Road (County Road 9435) and proceed for 27.5 miles. Turn right on Deep Lake-Boundary Road (CR 9445) and continue for 7.25 miles to the abandoned mining district of Leadpoint. Turn right here onto graveled Silver Creek Road (CR 4720), which becomes Forest Road 7078 after 1.5 miles. In another 0.4 mile bear left at a Y-junction (the right fork leads to South Fork Silver Creek,

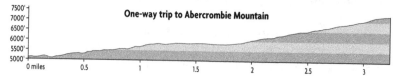

One-way trip to Abercrombie Mountain

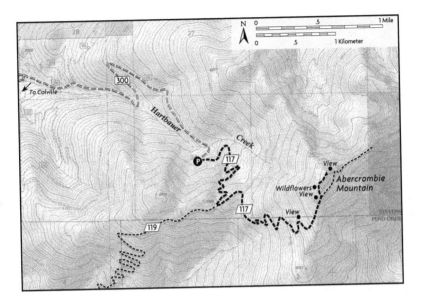

Hike 28). Follow this road, FR 7078, (signed "Abercrombie Mountain Trailhead 7 miles") for 4.4 miles. Turn right onto FR 300 (signed "Trailhead 3.5 miles"). This road is in decent shape for the first 2 miles, but deteriorates from there. High clearance is recommended. The trail begins at the end of the road.

One foot! Just 1 lousy foot is all that keeps this lofty peak from being eastern Washington's highest summit. That honor goes to nearby Gypsy Peak. Still, this summit is impressive—the views are grand, the meadows resplendent! And Abercrombie is a lot easier to get to than Gypsy. So although this peak is 1 foot shy of being eastern Washington's number one summit, it's still a great feat to tackle, by two feet or four.

The hike to the 7308-foot summit is short, but steep in sections. Except for a few rocky places near the top, the tread is good. For the first mile water is readily available, but beyond that it's a pretty dry hike. Hike this on a cool day, especially when the skies are clear. The view from this summit is extensive, from the Cascades to the Selkirks, the Monashees to the Purcells, the Pend Oreille River to the Columbia, and the Kootenay Valley all the way to the Columbia Plateau.

The trail begins on an old logging road. After following this alder-lined route for 1.4 miles the two of you will emerge at a junction (5200 ft.). Take the trail left to the summit. The trail right travels downhill

Makeshift shelter built by visitors on Abercrombie Mountain summit

for almost 6 miles to Silver Creek. (If you can arrange for a shuttle, it makes for a nice one-way hike off the mountain.) The trail begins to steepen. Forest soon yields to meadows, and the views expand with each contour crossed.

At 3 miles you'll reach the junction with the Flume Creek Trail, which drops steeply down the east side of the mountain. Continue on, making the last 0.25-mile climb to the rocky summit, where you'll find the ruins of an old fire tower (be aware of sharp debris) and a monster cairn that adds 6 feet to Abercrombie's elevation. But no matter how high this mountain is, the views stand tall.

Some familiar peaks can be made out in the distance. The prominent mountain to the northwest is Old Glory. The Kettle Crest dominates the western horizon. Hall Mountain lies directly to the east. Gypsy Peak, supreme mountain of these parts, is just to the north of Hall.

28. South Fork Silver Creek

Location: Selkirk Mountains
Round Trip: 14 miles
Hiking Time: 7 hours
High Point: 5400 feet
Elevation Gain: 2200 feet
Maps: USGS Deep Lake, Metaline
Best Hiking Time: late May to mid-October
Contact: Colville National Forest, Colville Ranger District,
(509) 684-7000

Driving Directions: From the junction of US Highway 395 and State Route 20 in Colville, Washington, travel east on SR 20 for 1.1 miles. Across from the airport turn left on Aladdin Road (County Road 9435) and proceed for 27.5 miles. Turn right on Deep Lake-Boundary Road (CR 9445) and continue for 7.25 miles to the abandoned mining district of Leadpoint. Turn right here onto graveled Silver Creek Road (CR 4720), which becomes Forest Road 7078 after 1.5 miles. In another 0.4 mile bear right at a Y-junction (signed "South Fork Silver Creek Trailhead 2 miles"). Follow this road, FR 7078-070, 1.75 miles to a small campground. The trail begins from the southeast corner near a small clearing.

The longest and loneliest trail in the 32,000-acre Abercrombie-Hooknose Roadless Area, the South Fork Silver Creek Trail is also perhaps the easiest. Through a lovely valley, up a series of well-graded switchbacks, and along a scenic ridge, this trail climbs 2200 feet in 7 miles. From its terminus on Gunsight Pass—a U-shaped notch high on the ridge—it's an easy cross-country scramble to either Sherlock Peak to the south, Linton Mountain to the east, or Abercrombie Mountain to the north. But you don't have to go all the way to the pass or to these peaks to enjoy this trail. The first 2 miles along the South Fork

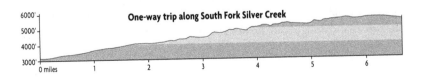

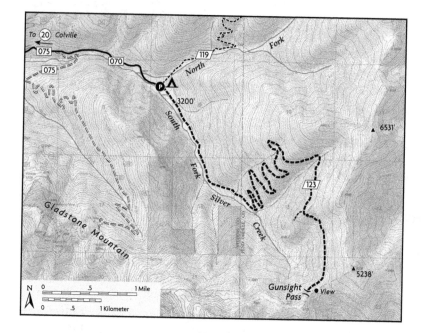

Silver Creek make for an easy hike, perfect during dreary weather or before the snows melt in the higher elevations.

The trail begins in a small campground, a good place to base if you want to check out the area's other trails. Utilizing an old jeep road, the trail begins along the creek and cuts through a lovely forest of larch, hemlock, birch, and poplar. In early season the forest floor blazes with pink and white trilliums. Yellow violets add their touch, too.

After 1 mile you'll cross the creek, and in another mile you'll cross the creek again. The log crossing is a bit iffy, so you may want to follow your pup through the water, if it's not too deep.

The trail soon leaves the old road and follows the creek for another 0.5 mile, passing through a lovely aspen grove before turning left along a tributary and climbing. The roar of Silver Creek fades as the trail ascends the ridge in 2.5 miles and nine switchbacks, crossing small creeks that may be dry by late summer.

After 5 miles of heavily forested hiking, the views begin. At 6 miles a short spur leads right to an open ledge with great views of nearby Sherlock Peak, BC's Rossland Range, and the Kettle Crest. This is a good spot to call it a day.

If you're intent on shooting for Gunsight Pass, follow the trail for 1

South Fork Silver Creek

mile more. It's a slightly downhill course through alpine forest and over open ledges before the trail peters out in the notch. A reliable stream crosses the trail 5 minutes from the spur-junction. Beyond that, water is scarce but views remain abundant.

29. Sullivan Lake

Location: Selkirk Mountains
Round Trip: 8.2 miles
Hiking Time: 3–4 hours
High Point: 2850 feet
Elevation Gain: 250 feet
Map: USGS Metaline Falls
Best Hiking Time: April to November
Contact: Colville National Forest, Sullivan Lake Ranger District, (509) 446-7500
Note: Dogs are not allowed on the beach at East Sullivan Campground.

Driving Directions: From Metaline Falls, Washington, drive 2 miles north on State Route 31. Turn right onto Sullivan Lake Road (County Road 9345), continuing 4.7 miles before turning left onto FR 22, signed "Salmo Mountain and East Sullivan Lake Campground." Proceed 0.4 mile, then turn right onto the access spur to the East Sullivan Lake Campground. The trailhead is 0.25 mile further on your left. The trail can also be accessed from the Noisy Creek Campground on the south end of Sullivan Lake, 8 miles from Ione via the Sullivan Lake Road.

Here's a great hike for a warm spring day or a cool autumn afternoon. With an elevation of just 2575 feet, Sullivan Lake provides a long hiking

Sullivan Lake, visible from much of the Lakeshore Trail

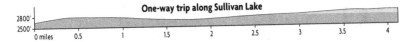

One-way trip along Sullivan Lake

season. Summer is a good time to visit, too, for there are plenty of places to take a dip in one of northeastern Washington's largest mountain lakes.

The Lakeshore Trail travels along the entire eastern shore of Sullivan Lake and along the base of hovering Hall Mountain. It connects two fine lakeside campgrounds, and a weekend car camp trip to Sullivan makes for great hiking and paddling right from camp.

The hike here is described from north to south, but it doesn't really matter which end of the lake you begin from. You'll be returning in the opposite direction either way. Lakeshore Trail 504 begins in forest and slowly climbs to a scenic bluff, one of several that offer sweeping views of the lake. En route to the bluff you'll pass two short side trails. The trail to the left makes a little nature loop. The trail to the right goes directly to the East Sullivan Campground.

From the bluff the trail enters a cool forest of cedar, fir, and hemlock, and crosses Hall Creek (often dry by late summer). After a short descent back to lake level the trail continues through a lovely forest dominated by birch (reminiscent of my native New Hampshire). Hidden coves and quiet beaches make for great lunch, swim, and nap spots.

The well-built trail crosses Noisy Creek (which is pretty quiet by late summer) before climbing to another scenic bluff. It's then a short descent to a peaceful cove and a final push to its southern terminus at the Noisy Creek Campground. At Noisy Creek (your pal should be leashed in the campground), fill your water bottles, go for another swim, then return, enjoying the entire 4.1-mile trail all over again.

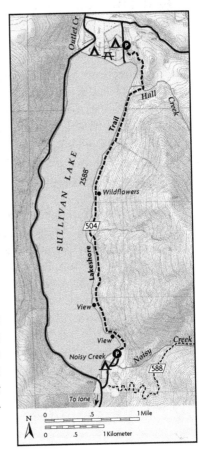

30. Noisy Creek–Hall Mountain

Location: Selkirk Mountains
Round Trip up Creek Valley: 6.5 miles/to Hall Mountain: 14 miles
Hiking Time: 3–4 hours
High Point: 4400 feet
Elevation Gain: 1900 feet
Hiking Time: 7–8 hours
High Point: 6323 feet
Elevation Gain: 4000 feet
Maps: USGS Metaline Falls, Pass Creek
Best Hiking Time: April to November
For Hall Mountain: June to October
Contact: Colville National Forest, Sullivan Lake Ranger District, (509) 446-7500

Driving Directions: From Newport, Washington, follow State Route 20 north (west) 47 miles to the junction with SR 31 in Tiger. Continue north on SR 31 for 2 miles to the junction (0.5 mile south of Ione) with Sullivan Lake Road (County Road 9345). Turn right (east) on Sullivan Lake Road, cross the Pend Oreille River, and proceed 8 miles to the Noisy Creek Campground. Follow signs for Noisy Creek Trail, which begins in a day-use area in the campground.

If your sole intent is to summit Hall Mountain, then this hike is not for you. From July 1 to mid-August each year the Forest Service allows you to drive up the Johns Creek Road to a point high on the ridge that runs from Hall to Grassy Top. From this access, the hike to meadowy Hall Mountain is a mere 2.5 miles, with only 1000 feet of elevation gain. The rest of the year you can access this stunning summit only via two much longer routes. One is as dry as a bowl of kibble. The other, the Noisy Creek

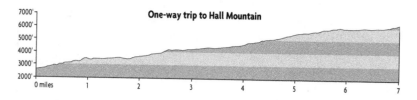

One-way trip to Hall Mountain

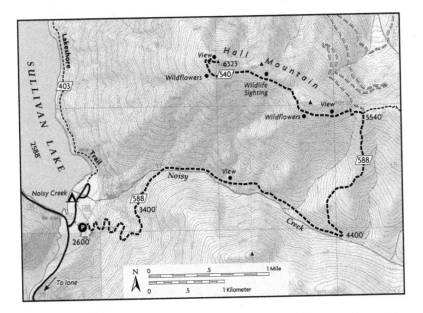

Trail, travels through cool forest and along a mountain stream for a portion of its sojourn.

It's still a long hike to the summit of Hall via this trail, and 4000 feet of elevation is no small task. However, the climb isn't too demanding. There are only a few short, steep sections, and there's plenty of shade. You'll likely have the summit to yourselves.

The Forest Service keeps the short trail option closed for most of the year to assure that few people (and few dogs) congregate on this mountain. Why? Hall is the home to a large population of bighorn sheep, and its sprawling alpine meadows have also played host to wayward grizzlies. No need to worry too much about the grizzlies—they are extremely rare in northeastern Washington. You are, however, almost guaranteed to see other wild critters here. Your dog should not hassle the sheep—but you already know that.

If you and Spot feel like tired old dogs and have no desire to reach Hall by such a long route, the first couple of miles up Noisy Creek still make for a good hike, especially early or late in the season.

Trail 588 leaves the campground and immediately begins climbing long switchbacks. The trail steadily gains elevation through a birch and fir forest. In about 1.25 miles the forest thins, providing nice views of Sullivan Lake (Hike 29). The trail eases and in 1.75 miles drops into a

Wildflowers below the summit of Hall Mountain

cool ravine where Noisy Creek must be forded (use caution in the spring). Before crossing the creek though, be sure to check out the old miner's cabin off to the left.

For the next 1.5 miles the trail follows Noisy Creek. Cedar groves and small cascades set the stage. On a hot day this is the place to be. Approximately 3.25 miles from the trailhead the trail turns northward up Hall, leaving the creek behind. This is the last available water and a good place to turn around if you're not intent on summiting.

Otherwise proceed for another 2 miles to the ridge and a junction (5540 ft.). Turn left (west) and continue for another 1.8 miles, climbing just under 700 feet to the summit. Almost the entire way is through meadows. The view down to Sullivan Lake and out to Crowell Ridge is breathtaking. Be sure to spend some time scanning your immediate surroundings—there's lots of resident wildlife on this summit and adjacent ridges. Be sure, too, that your dog watches her step near the summit, because sharp fire tower remains are scattered about.

31. Grassy Top Mountain

Location: Selkirk Mountains
Round Trip: 8 miles
Hiking Time: 4 hours
High Point: 6375 feet
Elevation Gain: 1000 feet
Map: USGS Pass Creek
Best Hiking Time: late June through October
Contact: Colville National Forest, Sullivan Lake Ranger District,
   (509) 446-7500

Driving Directions: From Metaline Falls, Washington, drive 2 miles north on State Route 31. Turn right onto Sullivan Lake Road (County Road 9345). Continue on this road for 4.75 miles before turning left (east) onto Forest Road 22, signed "Salmo Mountain." Follow this gravel road for 6 miles to a junction with FR 2220 just after a bridge crossing Sullivan Creek. Turn right (south) and continue on a much rougher FR 22 (signed "To Priest Lake") for 7.75 miles to a small pull-off at Pass Creek Pass. Park here and walk a few hundred feet west along the road to the trailhead, signed "Grassy Top Trail No. 503."

A peak named Grassy Top? What graminivorous (I did not make this word up!) canine can resist hiking to this herbaceous heaven? With only 1000 feet of mellow climbing, I can't imagine too many can. The trail to Grassy Top is one of the easiest ridge hikes in this book, suitable for young pups, old hounds, and every age in between. However, there's no water along the way, so be sure that you're both well-equipped.

The trip to Grassy Top is straightforward. Starting with a short drop from the road, the trail enters an old-growth forest of spruce and fir. It soon crosses the headwaters of Pass Creek. Other than lingering snow, this will be your only water along the way.

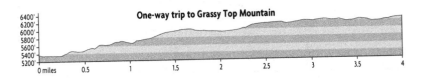

One-way trip to Grassy Top Mountain

Angling around some ledges, the trail begins to climb in a series of long and gentle switchbacks. After 1.5 miles the brunt of the climb is finished. It's now a pleasurable hike along a ridge that reaches between 6000 and 6200 feet. The forest thins, offering limited views eastward. In 2.7 miles you come to a junction with Trail 533, which leads 7 dry miles to Hall Mountain.

Proceed left, continuing on Trail 503. Not far from the junction the trail enters an expansive meadow, allowing an unobstructed view of one of northeastern Washington's least known major peaks, Molybdenite Mountain. There are good views, too, of the entire Grassy Top-Hall Mountain Roadless Area. Scan the unbroken forests and sprawling alpine meadows and wonder why this area has not yet been classified as a federal wilderness area.

After 1 mile of meadow marching (on the trail of course), you and Fido will emerge on the round, rather unexciting, grassy summit of Grassy Top

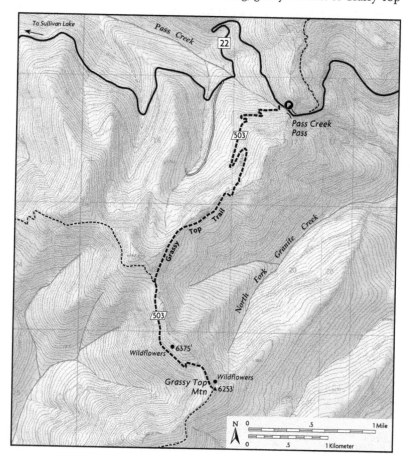

Snag along the ridge leading to Grassy Top Mountain

Mountain (6253 ft.). This ending may seem anticlimactic. If so, retrace your steps 5 minutes or so to an unmarked trail that takes off north from the main trail. Here you'll find a short, steep path that climbs 200 feet to a 6375-foot knoll. The views are even better than those from the main summit, especially to the north of the Shedroof Divide in the Salmo-Priest Country.

32. Thunder Mountain Loop

Location: Selkirk Mountains, Salmo-Priest Wilderness
Round Trip: 14 miles
Hiking Time: 8 hours
High Point: 6200 feet
Elevation Gain: 2000 feet, with some additional ups and downs
Maps: USGS Salmo Mt., Helmer Mt.
Best Hiking Time: late June to mid-October
Contact: Colville National Forest, Sullivan Lake Ranger District, (509) 446-7500

Driving Directions: From Metaline Falls, Washington, drive 2 miles north on State Route 31. Turn right onto County Road 9345 and head towards Sullivan Lake. Just before the lake (4.7 miles from SR 31) turn left onto Forest Road 22. Follow this gravel road east for 6 miles. Where FR 22 bears right to Pass Creek Pass (just after the bridge crossing Sullivan

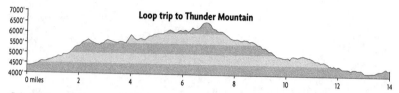

Creek), bear left onto FR 2220 and continue 6 miles to the Thunder Creek Trailhead located across from the Gypsy Meadows Camping Area.

This is a great loop into some of the loneliest country in northeastern Washington. Although you'll hike 7 miles along the lofty Shedroof Divide, the views are limited. The solitude is what makes this trek. You'll probably be alone, except for other four-legged critters. This is bear country and your buddy will pick up on that immediately. There is an exceptional amount of bear sign in this area, so use caution and keep your furry friend close by.

However, it's not the bears that are the main concern on this hike. It's the lack of water. It's plentiful at both ends of the hike, but come late July this stretch along the Shedroof can be waterless. You'll need to pack a few quarts for the two of you, especially if you plan on camping halfway, near the tempting slopes of Thunder Mountain.

I prefer to do this loop clockwise, getting the 0.5-mile road walk out of the way. From the Thunder Creek Trailhead walk up FR 2220, by Gypsy Meadows, (mosquito heaven in early summer) to Shedroof Cut-off Trail 511, which travels 1.75 steep miles to the Shedroof Divide. One mile up the trail, Sullivan Creek must be crossed. This may be difficult in high water, but enjoyable in hot weather. After 2.25 miles you'll access Shedroof Divide Trail 512 (5500 ft.).

From this point travel south for 6.5- lonely and lofty miles. The route is mostly through subalpine forest with bear grass lining the way. Occasional openings give extended views south to the Grassy Top Roadless Area and over massive Priest Lake to the Idaho Selkirk Range.

At about 7 miles the trail rounds Thunder Mountain, staying below the summit. Here you'll find some small campsites near an unreliable spring. Look for the old spur trail leading 0.5 mile to the summit. If you spend the evening, a quick trip to the old lookout site is worth the effort. Your dog won't have much difficulty and you'll both relish the breeze and views from the 6560-foot summit.

Continue along the Shedroof Divide and come to a somewhat obscure junction with Trail 311. This trail drops off the ridge to Idaho and

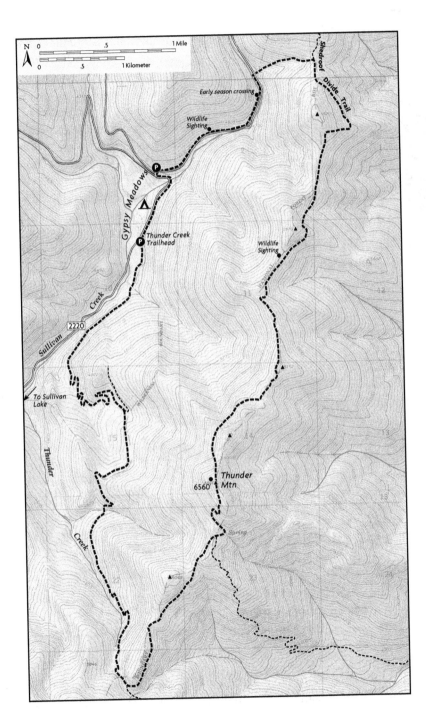

N 0 .5 1 Mile
0 .5 1 Kilometer

Shedroof Divide Trail

Early season crossing

Wildlife Sighting

P

Gypsy Meadows

Thunder Creek Trailhead

Wildlife Sighting

Sullivan Creek

2220

To Sullivan Lake

Thunder Creek

Thunder Mtn
6560'

Spring

View toward Upper Priest Lake region in Idaho, from Shedroof Divide north of Thunder Mountain

oblivion. About 8.75 miles from your start you'll intersect Thunder Creek Trail 526 on your right. Take this trail and begin your descent off the Divide. This is one of my favorite trails in the Salmo-Priest Wilderness. You'll be greeted by giant cedars and hemlocks, some of the finest specimens in all of eastern Washington. Resembling a Cascade Mountains forest, it's cool and invigorating. After about a mile of descending, you'll come to Thunder Creek. Your dog will want to belly flop in it, while you'll want to soak your bandana.

Enjoy this beautiful old-growth forest, because after 3 miles on the Thunder Creek Trail (11.75 miles from the start) you'll leave the wilderness and enter an area of old cuts. The last 2.25 miles are on a gentle old road with views out toward Gypsy Peak. It can be a hot walk during midsummer, but there's always another opportunity to soak in Sullivan Creek back at the trailhead.

33. Salmo Loop–Little Snowy Top

Location: Selkirk Mountains, Salmo-Priest Wilderness
Round Trip: 20 miles
Hiking Time: 2 days
High Point: 6829 feet
Elevation Gain: 3600 feet
Maps: USGS Salmo Mt., Continental Mt.
Best Hiking Time: July to mid-October
Contact: Colville National Forest, Sullivan Lake Ranger District, (509) 446-7500

Driving Directions: From Metaline Falls, Washington, drive 2 miles north on State Route 31. Turn right onto County Road 9345 and head towards Sullivan Lake. Just before the lake (4.7 miles from SR 31) turn left onto Forest Road 22 and follow it east for 6 miles. Where FR 22 bears right to Pass Creek Pass (just after the bridge crossing Sullivan Creek), bear left onto FR 2220 and continue for 13 more miles to its end at the trailhead for Salmo Basin Trail 506 and Salmo Divide Trail 535.

This is one of the finest wilderness hikes in eastern Washington (okay, technically northern Idaho, too). This 20-mile loop takes you deep into the Salmo-Priest Wilderness, the only federal wilderness area in northeastern Washington. Within these nearly 40,000 acres are some of the last roaming grounds in the Evergreen State for grizzly, mountain caribou, wolf, and wolverine. The adjacent wildlands in Idaho (17,600 acres under consideration for federal wilderness) are also prime habitat for the aforementioned species.

You'd be extremely fortunate to even catch a glimpse of one of these elusive creatures. What you will see along this hike though is rugged alpine scenery, incredible vistas of the surrounding Selkirk peaks, miles of wildflower-laden meadows, and one of the most impressive old-growth cedar forests this side of the Cascades.

For you and your dog this loop offers the opportunity to spend a few nights out in a wild corner of the Inland Northwest. Although you can easily do this hike in two days, consider a few extra days for side trips to summits or just more time by the river. The trails that compose the loop are well maintained, and the grades along the ridge and into the Salmo Basin are gentle. There's plenty of water—this corner of Washington receives almost 60 inches of rain each year, making it the wettest spot in the Evergreen State east of the Cascades. However, the second half of the loop tends to be dry come late summer, so you will need to haul a few extra quarts once you leave the Salmo River Basin. Keep in mind that the Salmo River can have a little too much water early in the season, making its crossing tricky.

The loop starts on Salmo Basin Trail 506, descending for 3 miles and dropping 1800 feet to the South Salmo River (4100 ft.) on a gentle grade.

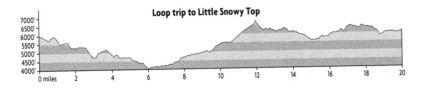

Loop trip to Little Snowy Top

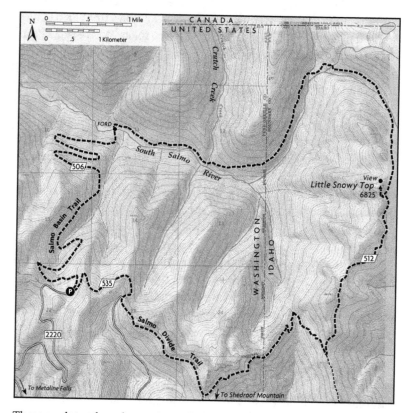

There are lots of creek crossings along the way. About halfway down the big cedars begin.

Ford the Salmo and come to a junction. The trail left is a long-abandoned path to the Canadian border. The loop continues right. Slowly regaining lost elevation, the trail traverses a magnificent forest of ancient giants. The river is always nearby, and there are plenty of good campsites. In 4.5 miles you'll cross Crutch Creek, followed in 0.7 mile by a well-marked trail junction. The trail right drops 0.3 mile to the river and to an old cabin. Good but well-used campsites surround the area.

Continue on Trail 506, crossing into Idaho in about a mile. The cedars and hemlocks soon yield to subalpine firs and Engelmann spruce, indicating that you're getting into higher country. At 6.5 miles you'll come to a good campsite just above the river. In 8 miles you'll cross a creek, your last reliable water source for the next 5 miles. In 9 miles you'll reach Snowy Top Pass on the Shedroof Divide (6200 ft.). This is a good place to base if you plan on summiting Snowy Top Mountain, but it's dry. Although this 7572-foot peak lacks any formal trail, the summit is easily attained by most fit hikers and hounds.

For the loop, continue on Trail 512. Ten miles from your start you'll come to the junction with the trail to Little Snowy Top Mountain. Take this 0.5-mile spur to the old lookout. Here you'll be rewarded with some of the finest views offered along this loop. Gaze out at Priest Lake and the jagged Idaho Selkirks. Admire the rolling green Shedroof Divide. Marvel at the pointy peaks around British Columbia's Kootenay Pass. There's a small campsite at the summit. The lookout is open, but the mice will probably drive your dog crazy (not to mention you!).

Retrace your steps to Trail 512 and continue along on one of the supreme ridge walks of the Inland Northwest. Stare down at the Priest River valley, a dizzying 4000 feet below you to the east as you traverse miles of meadows.

At 13.5 miles you'll come to some good campsites and a small creek. Make sure to rehydrate here, because water remains scarce the rest of the way. You'll now have to climb 700 feet as you cross back into Washington and approach a little notch between 6764-foot Shedroof Mountain and an unnamed 6682-foot peak.

Sailor enjoys the view.

With the climbing done and 17 miles behind you, you'll come to a junction with the Salmo Divide Trail 535. Turn right (north) and make one last small climb. On a mostly downhill course—with good views west down the Sullivan River drainage and limited views east to the territory you just explored—you'll eventually return to your vehicle at the trailhead.

If you want a great view of all of that Salmo-Priest Country the two of you just hiked, drive to the nearby Salmo Mountain Lookout on your way out. Your dog may even appreciate the huckleberries while you're waxing nostalgic about your expedition.

34. Bead Lake

Location: Selkirk Mountains
Round Trip: 10 miles
Hiking Time: 6 hours
High Point: 3200 feet
Elevation Gain: 400 feet
Map: USGS Bead Lake
Best Hiking Time: late April to November
Contact: Colville National Forest, Newport Ranger District, (509) 447-7300

Driving Directions: From Newport, Washington, head east on US Highway 2 to Old Town, Idaho. Immediately upon crossing the Pend Oreille River turn left (north) onto Le Clerc Creek Road (County Road 9305). In 1.5 miles reenter Washington. In 2.75 miles, bear right on Bead Lake Road (CR 3029). In 6 miles, just after entering the Colville National Forest, turn right on Bead Lake Ridge Road (Forest Road 3215) and follow it 0.6 mile to the trailhead.

Lying just a few miles outside of the pastoral Pend Oreille River valley, large and mostly undeveloped, Bead Lake is a pleasant surprise. It is surrounded by groves of old growth, it has no visible outlet, and its shoreline is graced with a beautifully constructed hiking trail. Furthermore, this pleasant trail rarely sees large numbers of users, unlike the Sullivan Lake Trail to the north.

Sheltered by a thick forest canopy, the Bead Lake Trail is perfect for rainy or sweltering hot days. There are lots of places to camp along the

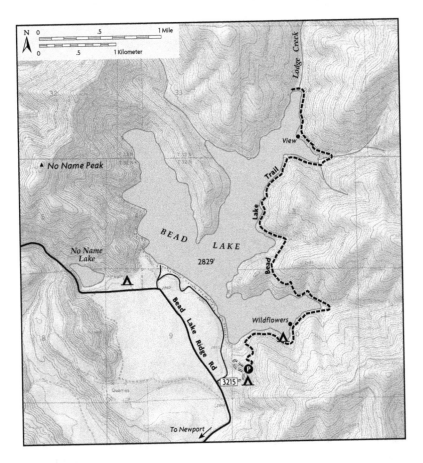

way, and the snow melts out early, making this trail ideal for early- and late-season backpacking trips. The spring flowers are profuse, but so are the ticks. Be sure to perform regular scans on both you and your dog.

The trail starts in a cool forest of cedar and fir, immediately dropping to the boat launch. Utilizing an old road for about 0.5 mile, you'll pass a nice but busy campsite just before the real trail begins. Dropping closer to the lake, the trail emerges on an open ledge. Enjoy the sparkling blue-green waters and the dazzling floral show, including the calypso orchids.

In 1.5 miles you'll come to the Enchantment Campsite tucked into a

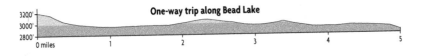

One-way trip along Bead Lake

Bead Lake seen from Bead Lake Trail

dense forest of cedar, followed by a dry forest of ponderosa pine. Begin climbing about 200 feet over a ridge to bypass a finger of land jutting into the lake. In 2.5 miles descend to the inviting shoreline, where quiet coves and secluded groves await. In 4 miles you'll reach a spectacular grove of giant cedars and western white pines, including one pine that measures 15 feet, 7 inches in circumference.

At 5 miles you'll come to a trail junction and yet another inviting cedar grove, this one dissected by Lodge Creek, one of the main tributaries into the lake. This is a good spot to turn around or to consider spending the night. From this spot the Bead Lake Spur Trail 127.1 crosses Lodge Creek and peters out in about 0.5 mile on the lake's northwestern shoreline. The Bead Lake Trail continues for another 1.4 miles, following the creek and climbing 500 feet to FR 3215.

COLUMBIA PLATEAU

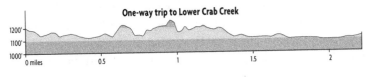

35. Blythe and Chukar Lakes

Location: Columbia Plateau
Round Trip: 5 miles
Hiking Time: 3 hours
High Point: 1250 feet
Elevation Gain: 350 feet
Best Hiking Time: late March through May
Map: USGS O'Sullivan Dam
Contact: Columbia National Wildlife Refuge, (509) 466-2668
Notes: Dogs must be leashed. The refuge is closed October 1 to the end of February.

Driving Directions: From Spokane, Washington, drive west on Interstate 90 to Moses Lake. Take exit 179 heading south for 10 miles on State Route 17. Turn right (west) on SR 262 and proceed for 10 miles. At milepost 14 (directly across from the Mar Don Resort) turn left onto a gravel road signed for public fishing, Blythe, Corral, and Chukar Lakes. Pass Corral Lake and entering the Columbia National Wildlife Refuge in 1.3 miles. The road ends in 1.7 miles at Blythe Lake. The trail begins behind a gate in the southeast corner of the parking lot.

The Columbia National Wildlife Refuge is a bird-watchers paradise. It's a land of incredible natural diversity and provides important habitat for

One-way trip to Lower Crab Creek

```
1200'
1100'
1000'
   0 miles        0.5              1            1.5            2
```

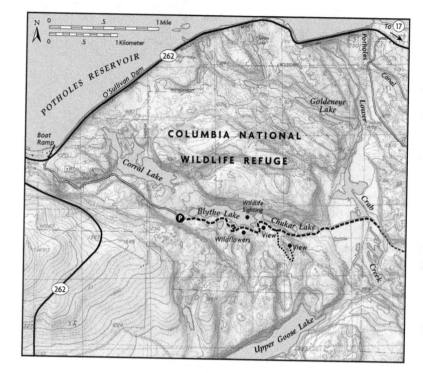

both breeding and migratory birds. Composed of basaltic coulees littered with lakes and marshes, it's an oasis in the driest part of the Inland Northwest. This region, known as the Channeled Scablands, was formed by ancient cataclysmic floods. The Columbia National Wildlife Refuge protects almost 30,000 acres of this enchanting landscape.

You and your dog will love exploring it, but only if you visit during the spring. Summer is just too hot. Fall is hunting season and winter is breeding season. Ticks can be a problem come May. Rattlesnakes rarely venture out in the cold and they're quite elusive the rest of the year. Nevertheless, don't let Rover go sniffing around in the basaltic talus slopes. Most importantly, the refuge was established for protecting wildlife; therefore, you and ol' Scratch should be on your best behavior.

The trail begins on an old road. After 0.5 mile of easy walking along enchanting Blythe Lake, make a sharp right turn on a fairly worn trail that leads up to the bench above the lake. Enjoy views of Blythe and the surrounding coulee. Continue walking eastward on good trail for about 10 minutes until you come to another old road-turned-trail. Remember this unimposing junction for the return. Continue left (east), hiking towards a beautiful basaltic cliff face. After 10 more minutes you'll reach a small hillcrest. Chukar Lake comes into view below. Follow the road-trail down to smaller Scaup Lake.

Note that the road-trail intersects another road-trail just before Scaup. Take the left turn. Remember this junction, marked by a bird feeder, for the return trip. Now enjoy a virtually flat hike past Scaup and to the extensive wetlands of Crab Creek, part of the Marsh Unit I and II restoration project. Go straight through a four-way junction and continue east on the main trail. There are lots of road-trails branching off, allowing for hours of extensive exploring.

This hike alone, however, should keep the both of you quite content. Continue past the small "dam" until the road-trail begins to climb out of the coulee. This is a good turnaround, about 2.5 miles from the trailhead. The trail continues another mile to a parking lot located off of the road that skirts the eastern perimeter of the refuge.

Take time to enjoy the wildlife. Your dog will probably be enthralled by all of the jumping frogs; you'll be impressed by the avocets, terns, quails, geese, and the myriad of songbirds and ducks.

Return the way you came. The boat launch at Blythe makes for a great swim spot. Nearby Potholes State Park makes for a good overnight option, allowing the two of you another day to explore even more of this intriguing wildlife refuge.

Frost on the plateau above Blythe Lake

36. Dusty Lake

Location: Columbia Plateau
Round Trip: 3 miles
Hiking Time: 2 hours
High Point: 1200 feet
Elevation Loss: 400 feet
Best Hiking Time: March to May
Map: USGS Babcock Ridge
Contact: Quincy Wildlife Area, (509) 754-4624 or (509) 764-6641
Notes: The road is closed from October 1 to January 1, requiring a 1.7-mile walk to the trailhead. A Washington Department of Fish and Wildlife vehicle-use permit is required.

Driving Directions: From Moses Lake, Washington, drive west on Interstate 90 to exit 151. Follow State Route 281 north 4.5 miles to a junction with White Trail Road. (**Note:** If coming from the west, take exit 149 to SR 281; reach White Trail Road in 5.6 miles.) Turn left and follow this paved road for 3 miles. At a curve, turn left on a road signed for fishing and hunting. Continue 2.2 miles to Dusty Lake Trailhead on your right.

Although the hot and arid Columbia Plateau isn't exactly an ideal place to take Rover, there are some good destinations among the sage and steppe. The 15,000-acre Quincy Lakes State Wildlife Area is one of them. Here, scattered about in the striking basalt canyons along the Columbia River, are scores of little lakes, creeks, and waterfalls. The entire area is a haven for birds, and the lakes support fish. It's a great area to explore, but there are a few precautions.

It's best to hike Quincy Lakes in the spring, before the stifling heat of summer. Winter can be nice, too—snowfall is light—but it can get pretty windy and cold. Water is abundant, but it's best to keep your buddy from drinking it because of the agricultural runoff. Wildflowers proliferate

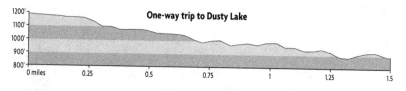

One-way trip to Dusty Lake

come April, but so do ticks. There are rattlesnakes, but they're pretty shy and during the cooler months it's unlikely you'll ever see (or hear) one. Finally, this is an active hunting area, so be aware of the seasons and plan accordingly.

The hike to Dusty Lake is short and sweet. You begin by hiking down off a bluff and through a terraced canyon. Immediately drop from the trailhead and cross a bridge over a swift creek lined with willows. Emerge to a lookout. Directly below is a beaver pond, fed by a crashing cascade. Continue down into the canyon, cross the creek once more and then forever lose it as it disappears into the basalt.

Soon the lake comes into view from a nice bluff midway down the canyon. You must help your dog negotiate two spots. Short-legged pooches will need a lift; long-legged hounds will need a push. Otherwise it's pretty smooth sailing. In 1.5 miles you'll reach a lovely spot on the lake's eastern shore.

Pepper romps through the sagelands near Dusty Lake.

You could easily spend the afternoon here, but if you want to explore some more, there is a trail to the lake's western shore. However, a talus slope must be negotiated, making it less than ideal for many four-legged wanderers.

There is another way to reach the western shore, via a gated dirt road from the north end of the wildlife area. This makes for a hike more than twice as long but without the 400-foot climb necessary for the return trip on the regular trail.

BLUE MOUNTAINS

37. Tucannon River

Location: Blue Mountains
Round Trip: 9 miles
Hiking Time: 4 hours
High Point: 4100 feet
Elevation Gain: 600 feet
Maps: Wenaha-Tucannon Wilderness, Umatilla National Forest USFS
Best Hiking Time: May to November
Contact: Umatilla National Forest, Pomeroy Ranger District, (509) 843-1891
Note: A NW Forest Pass is required.

Driving Directions: From Pomeroy, Washington, head 4 miles west on US Highway 12, turn south on Tatman Mountain Road and proceed 9 miles to the Tucannon River Road. Continue south 14 miles on the Tucannon River Road, which becomes Forest Road 47. Just beyond Camp Wooten at the Tucannon River Bridge, bear left onto FR 4712 and follow it 4.5 miles to the trailhead. From Dayton head west on Patit Road for 14 miles, turn left onto the Hartsuck Grade and follow it 4 miles to the Tucannon River Road. Turn right on Tucannon River Road, following the above directions.

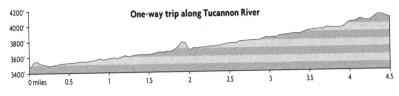

One-way trip along Tucannon River

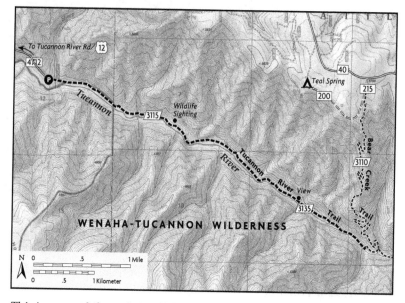

This is a great hike early in the season when the high country is still covered with snow and the surrounding hills haven't yet begun to fry in the hot Umatilla sun. But even when the mercury rises, the banks of the Tucannon are graced with cool forest. Mosses and ferns attest to this. It's a well-shaded path with plenty of places to soak your feet. If you're a dog, no reason to stop at the feet; nothing less than a full body plunge will suffice!

Although in some years you and Rover can set out on this trail in early May, it's not unusual for winter storms to lay a few obstacles in your path. While the occasional downed tree may be a hindrance to you, to your pup it's a play park.

With the river always within earshot, the trail gains a mere 600 feet of elevation in its 4.5 miles. Surprisingly, the river is not within the 177,465-acre Wenaha-Tucannon Wilderness; however, the upper reaches of the Tucannon are still pristine and would make for a welcome addition to this wilderness area, the largest protected roadless area in southeastern Washington.

As with most of the Blue Mountain country, keep your eyes out for elk and wild turkeys. No doubt your dog will see them before you do. Rattlesnakes aren't too much of a concern on this trail, but there are a few open areas along the way where ledges reflect heat. In early season though, those same open areas won't rattle you. They'll dazzle you with floral shows starring white lupines.

Mittens easily crosses a 4-foot high log that blocks the trail.

Plenty of good campsites lie along the way. After 4.5 miles of some of the most enjoyable hiking in these parts, the trail terminates at a junction with the Bear Creek Trail. Either direction along this trail requires a 1500-foot climb with very little water. While you contemplate it, your dog's probably already heading back down the Tucannon River Trail hoping to stop again at her favorite spots. You should, too.

38. Oregon Butte Grand Loop

Location: Blue Mountains
Round Trip: 17 miles
Hiking Time: 2 days
High Point: 6387 feet
Elevation Gain: 3100 feet
Maps: Wenaha-Tucannon Wilderness, Umatilla National Forest USFS
Best Hiking Time: June to November
Contact: Umatilla National Forest, Pomeroy Ranger District, (509) 843-1891
Note: A NW Forest Pass is required.

Driving Directions: From Pomeroy, Washington, head 4 miles west on US Highway 12, turn south on Tatman Mountain Road, and proceed 9 miles to the Tucannon River Road. Continue south 14 miles on the Tucannon River Road, which becomes Forest Road 47. FR 47 splits into FR 4712 and FR 4713. Bear right on FR 4713 and follow it 2.5 miles to the Panjab Trailhead, a large area with restrooms, tables, and a corral. From Dayton head west on Patit Road for 14 miles, turn left onto the Hartsuck Grade and follow it 4 miles to the Tucannon River Road. Turn right on Tucannon River Road, following the above directions.

The Wenaha-Tucannon Wilderness protects 177,465 acres of forests, canyons, pristine rivers, and basaltic buttes in the remote Blue Mountains of Washington and Oregon. Hundreds of miles of trail traverse this wilderness, yet most see very little use. For you and your dog, solitude, superb wildlife viewing, and a quality backcountry experience are guaranteed.

Although you can traipse through the Wenaha-Tucannon Wilderness from late spring to late fall, it's best to avoid this area during the heart of summer. It is not unusual for the Blues to record temperatures in excess of

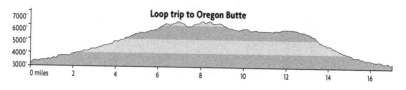

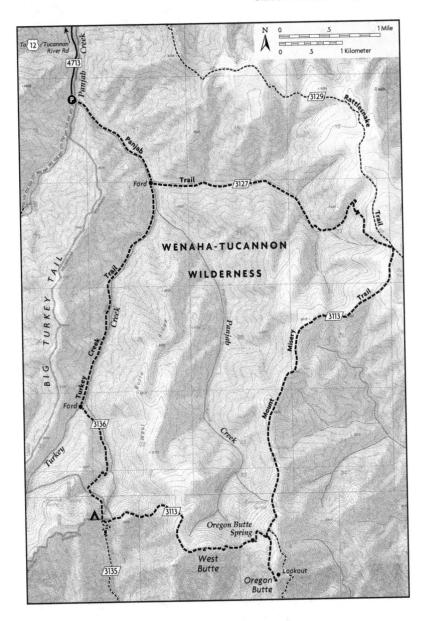

100°F. Surprisingly, they are not dry. Abundant springs can be found along the ridges and slopes, and numerous creeks and rivers drain the canyons. Autumn is the best time to explore, when the air is cool and the larches paint the hillsides golden. However, be advised that hunting is popular

Alan Bauer and Mittens cross the bridge over Panjab Creek.

here. Know when hunting season begins and be sure that you and your dog are sporting orange.

The Oregon Butte Grand Loop introduces you and your canine to some of the best aspects this wilderness has to offer: lush forests, tumbling creeks, alpine meadows, and sweeping views from the highest point in southeastern Washington. While the scenery keeps you satisfied, your dog will enjoy picking up on the scents of the wilderness's abundant and diverse fauna.

Panjab Trail 3127 immediately crosses Panjab Creek on a sturdy bridge and enters the Wenaha-Tucannon Wilderness. The first mile of this wide trail is a pure delight. The tread is soft, the terrain is flat, the creek is always nearby. The lush forest almost looks like it belongs in the Cascades. At a marked junction, turn right on Turkey Creek Trail 3136. The trail on your left is the continuation of the Panjab Trail, your return route.

Ford Turkey Creek, which in early summer may be difficult for both you and your dog. Once across, however, the two of you have miles of a beautiful canyon to travel. Lined with lush ferns and yews, the trail tunnels through an old-growth forest of firs. Plenty of creekside campsites are available.

Four miles from your start the trail crosses Turkey Creek (4600 ft.) and begins to climb out of the canyon. After 1 mile and 1000 vertical feet you'll arrive at the Teepee Campground (also accessed from FR Road 4608), temporarily leaving the wilderness. Enjoy good views south into the Butte Creek drainage before reentering the wilderness and resuming your loop by way of the Mount Misery Trail 3113 just east of the campground.

The next 6.5 miles are some of the finest trail in the entire Wenaha-Tucannon Wilderness. On a skyline route that never dips below 5500 feet, the trail snakes through alpine meadows, basaltic balds, and sprawling fir and larch forests. Sweeping canyon views punctuate the way. Several trailside springs provide aquatic relief. The hiking is pure pleasure for you and your pooch, for the grade is easy and the tread well groomed.

Two miles from the Teepee Campground (7 miles from the trailhead) come to the reliable Oregon Butte Spring. A quarter-mile beyond is the junction with the 0.5-mile spur to the Oregon Butte Lookout, a mandatory side trip for you and your intrepid dog. From this 6387-foot basaltic peak, the highest summit in southeastern Washington, views in the Blues don't get any better. A panorama of mountain and canyon country will keep you mesmerized. Your dog will probably be more interested in shade, opting to plop down beneath the lookout cabin.

When you tire of soaking up the scenery—and when your pal's ready to soak up some more scents—return to the main trail and continue east along the ridge. Three miles from Oregon Butte and 10 miles from your start you come to the serene open country known as Indian Corral (5700 ft.). A landscape of bald basaltic ledges and serene alpine meadows sprawls before you. It's an inviting place to set up camp and explore. Water can be obtained at Dunlap Spring just east of where the Mount Misery Trail 3113 meets Panjab Trail 3127 and Rattlesnake Trail 3129.

When the two of you are ready to return to civilization, follow Panjab Trail 3127 back to the trailhead. It's a 5.6-mile descent through cool forests and along babbling creeks. Upon completing the 17-mile loop, your buddy may want to take one last dip in Panjab Creek before napping in the flatbed for the long ride home.

39. Puffer Butte

Location: Blue Mountains
Round Trip: 2.5 miles
Hiking Time: 2 hours
High Point: 4550 feet
Elevation Gain: 450 feet
Best Hiking Time: April to November
Map: USGS Fields Spring
Contact: Washington State Parks and Recreation, (800) 233-0321
Notes: Dogs must be leashed. A Washington State Parks Pass is required.

Driving Directions: From the Lewiston-Clarkston area, drive south on Washington State Route 129 for 30 miles. About 4 miles past the tiny village of Anatone you'll see a large entrance sign for Fields Spring State Park. Turn left into the park and proceed to the large parking lot just before the campground. Locate a bulletin board and trailhead sign marked "Puffer Butte 1.1 miles."

Washington's southeast corner offers some of the most dramatic scenery in the entire state. This lightly visited area is a land of high plateaus, deep canyons, forested hills, and sweeping views that will mesmerize you and your best friend. Puffer Butte in Fields Spring State Park makes for a great introduction to this remote region.

This hike is short but the rewards are grand. If you desire an extension, the park also contains miles of forested track used primarily for winter skiing, which also make for nice walking paths. Consider spending the night here. Fields Spring offers peaceful camping under a cool canopy of pine and fir. The Puffer Butte Trail takes off right from the campground.

Puffer Butte sits at the eastern edge of the Blue Mountains, an area known for some of the best elk habitat in the state. During the fall

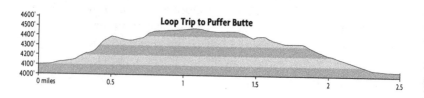

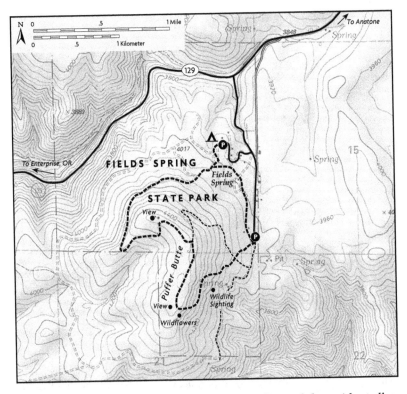

hunting season, Fields Spring offers you, your dog and the resident elk a safe haven from the flurry of activity in neighboring public lands.

From the trailhead elevation of 4100 feet you'll notice that the temperatures here are cooler than in the oft-sweltering Snake River valley. The hike to the butte is completely shaded. Prevalent winds will also help keep you and your dog from overheating. In the autumn and early spring it can be pretty brisk.

The trail begins in a mature forest of Douglas fir, ponderosa pine, and western larch. There are many fine, large specimens along the way. In 5 minutes you'll come to a signed junction. Stay right; you'll be returning on the trail to your left. As the trail works its way up the butte, it frequently crosses the roads that also serve as ski trails.

Fields Spring is teeming with grouse and wild turkey. Your four-legged hiking partner will probably be more aware of this than you. A keen and well-behaved pooch will help you scope these birds out. Keep your senses tuned for rustlings made by larger park residents. Elk and deer love these open forests.

An elk roams the upper meadows near the summit of Puffer Butte.

In about 40 minutes you'll reach the crest of the butte, at 4550 feet. The forest yields to open grassy slopes, providing fantastic views. Oregon's Wallowa Mountains rise on the southern horizon above the canyon cut by the Grande Ronde River. The Craig Mountains of Idaho hover east above the massive Snake River Canyon. Roam the butte for different perspectives. Be careful during spring, for anxious ticks may want to hitch a ride with you or your dog.

After you explore Puffer, descend via the Scout Trail, which heads east off the summit and then makes a sharp left turn back into the forest. You'll pass through a beautiful grove of ponderosa pines. Just before the Scout Trail ends in a parking lot, take the spur left to the Puffer Butte Environmental Learning Center (ELC). The trail continues behind the ELC's southwest corner. After a short climb you'll return to the intersection with the Puffer Butte Trail. Turn right. The parking lot and campground are 5 minutes away.

If you want more, the ski-trail roads await you.

SPOKANE COUNTY AND PALOUSE

40. Day Mountain Loop– Mount Spokane State Park

Location: Spokane County
Round Trip: 6 miles
Hiking Time: 3 hours
High Point: 5100 feet
Elevation Gain: 200 feet
Maps: USGS Mount Spokane, Mount Kit Carson
Best Hiking Time: June through October
Contact: Mount Spokane State Park, (509) 238-6845
Notes: Dogs must be leashed. A Washington State Parks Pass is required.

Driving Directions: From Spokane, Washington, follow US Highway 2 north for 10 miles to Mead. Follow State Route 206 east for 15 miles to Mount Spokane State Park. From Spokane Valley follow Argonne Road 8 miles north to SR 206. Turn right and proceed to the state park. Continue on the Mount Spokane Park Road 4.25 miles to the Bald Knob Picnic Area and Campground. The trail begins off the park road across from the entrance to the picnic area.

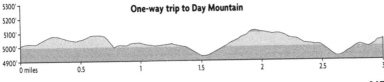

Rising above the Spokane Valley and neighboring Rathdrum Prairie, 5883-foot Mount Spokane is a prominent local landmark. A southern outpost of the Selkirk Mountains, it's also a local favorite spot for outdoor recreation, particularly for skiers and mountain bikers. There's plenty of room for hikers and their dogs, too, in this 13,800-acre park. The trip to Day Mountain, a shoulder of Mount Spokane, makes for an excellent hike.

With a trailhead that begins at 5000 feet and a destination just slightly higher, the elevation gain on this trip is minimal. Day Mountain is one of the quieter peaks in the park, and chances are you'll encounter only a handful of other trail users. And although the views from this summit are not quite as good as those from nearby Mount Kit Carson, Day's meadows are grander.

After the snow melts this trail is dry, so be sure to pack plenty of water for the two of you. However, take consolation in the fact that the sweat index is low on this hike. You can hydrate right at the start—piped water is available.

Trail 130 starts right across from the campground. The first mile is a pure delight, skirting nearly level beneath the summit of Mount Spokane

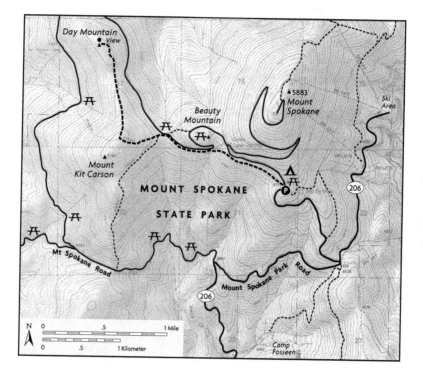

Open forest and bear grass line the trail to Day Mountain.

through an open forest offering teaser views of the countryside below. At a junction, turn left onto a fire road, also known as the Mount Kit Carson Loop Road. (The right-hand trail goes to an attractive CCC-constructed lodge that offers shelter and, in summer, water.) This is a popular bike route, so keep your pup close by. After a slight descent you'll come to a major trail junction complete with a privy (1.5 miles). Take the well-trodden trail that veers to the northwest, marked "Mt Kit Carson, Trails 170, 130, 115." After a stiff 10-minute climb you come to another junction. Continue right on Trails 170 and 130. Very soon afterwards you'll come to yet another junction—take the less obvious Trail 130, which heads right.

Now you're back on a quiet byway. No longer concerned about mountain bikers, you can enjoy the abundant birds while your pup can sniff out the moose nuggets along the trail. After a little bit of climbing you emerge into the meadows. As you crest the rounded summit of Day (2.5 miles) the meadows expand with the views. At a cairn that marks a sharp right-hand turn, leave the trail for the jumbled rocks on your left. This is the spot to feast on your Scooby Snacks and on the views—Steptoe Butte, the Kettles, the Pend Oreille country.

Return the way you came or continue on the trail to make a loop. Trail 130 heads back into the woods, dropping steeply, then emerging back on the Mount Kit Carson Loop Road (3 miles). Turn right (be sure to bear right again shortly afterward) and follow this route, gaining back some lost elevation to return to the privy junction (4.5 miles). It's 1.5 miles back to your vehicle from here.

Of course, if you and Fido want more exercise and views, you can always opt to hit the summits of Mount Kit Carson and Mount Spokane!

41. Iller Creek Conservation Area

Location: Spokane County
Round Trip: 2 miles
Hiking Time: 2 hours
High Point: 2800 feet
Elevation Gain: 400 feet
Maps: USGS Spokane SE
Best Hiking Time: March to November
Contact: Spokane County Parks Department, (509) 477-4730
Note: Dogs must be leashed.

Driving Directions: From Spokane Valley, Washington, take exit 287 off Interstate 90. Follow Argonne Road south, passing Sprague Ave. Argonne runs into Dishman Mica Road. Continue south. Turn right onto Schafer Road (the intersection is 3.5 miles from I-90). In a little less than a mile turn right onto 44th Avenue. Proceed 0.25 mile, turning left onto Farr Road, the second intersection. In 0.3 mile turn right on Holman Road. Continue on Holman for 0.75 mile. Just before the road makes a sharp left turn, park at a pull-out on the right in front of a gated dirt road. A large bulletin board announces the Iller Creek Conservation Area.

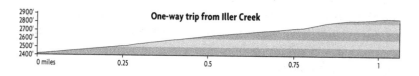

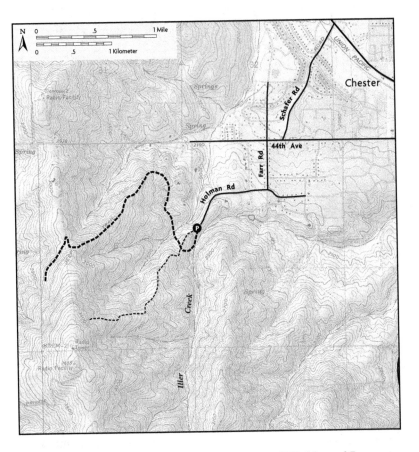

Spokane hikers have been enjoying the Dishman Hills Natural Resources Conservation Area (NCRA) for decades. With good trails and wildlife habitat just minutes from downtown Spokane, it's no surprise this is a popular place. But is it a good destination for Rover? Sure, you can bring your best friend out for a stroll here, but the two of you will have plenty of company, perhaps too much. So, here's a better plan. Just south of the NRCA is Iller Creek, a brand new 800-acre conservation area, courtesy of Spokane County Parks. It's twice as big as the NRCA, still within the Dishman Hills ecosystem, and contains miles of trails. Best of all, it gets a fraction of the visitors that the NRCA receives, making it a wonderful spot for you and Spot to enjoy nature.

So what's the catch? Why haven't the masses descended upon this place? Mainly because it is still a work in progress. A good portion of the property succumbed to fire in the early 1990s. The vegetation is coming

Trail along Iller Creek leading into the Iller Creek Conservation Area

back but erosion is a problem on the old firebreaks. Parks personnel will be rehabilitating slopes and constructing new trails. The best part of the property—an old timber road that travels along Iller Creek before climbing up onto the ridge—is not yet accessible. Parks officials are working on gaining access to it either by purchasing adjacent property or by acquiring an easement.

In the meanwhile you can still visit this area, which is open to the public. The best that you and your buddy can get right now is a nice short hike and a wonderful preview of what will ultimately become a prime hiking spot in Spokane Valley.

Hike past the gated dirt road just to the south of the parking area. Within a few minutes you come to a junction. Take the sharp right. (The left trail goes through private property—please respect it.) Traveling north, the trail traverses the old burn. The new forest is working hard. In spring plenty of wildflowers compensate for the lack of a green canopy. Continue on the main path and switchback to the south again. The views grow as you climb. Mount Spokane, Spokane Valley, and the Rathdrum Prairie unroll to the east. Continue climbing until you get to the edge of the property near the ridge crest. It's about a 1-mile hike from the parking area. If you want more, double back and explore some of the spur trails. It's best to explore this place early in the morning before the sun begins to beat down.

42. Liberty Lake Loop

Location: Spokane County
Round Trip: 6.5 miles
Hiking Time: 4 hours
High Point: 3250 feet
Elevation Gain: 1290 feet
Best Hiking Time: late April to November
Maps: USGS Mica Peak, Liberty Lake
Contact: Spokane County Parks Department, (509) 477-4730
Notes: Dogs must be leashed. There is a day-use fee of $2 per person
from mid-June through Labor Day.

Driving Directions: From Spokane, Washington, drive east on Interstate
90. Take exit 296 and proceed straight (east) through traffic lights onto
Appleway Avenue (Note sign: "Liberty Lake County Park 4.5 miles").
In 0.8 mile turn right on Molter Road. After another mile, turn left onto
Valley Way, which becomes Lakeside Road, for 2.5 miles to Zephyr Road.
Turn right on Zephyr. Enter the park in 0.25 mile and proceed to the
trailhead located within the campground. If the park gate is closed, park
at the gate and walk to the trailhead.

Tucked between the sprawling cities of Spokane and Post Falls is a 3000-acre
"pocket wilderness." Liberty Lake County Park straddles the Washington-
Idaho border, providing a green sliver to an ever-suburbanizing corridor.
Purchased for $245,000 in 1966, this 1-by-5-mile property is now a price-
less gem of the Spokane County Parks Department.

A mere 10 miles from downtown Spokane, you and your dog can
hike along rushing creeks, through old-growth forest, and to scenic
lookouts. Wildlife is abundant and viewing opportunities are good.

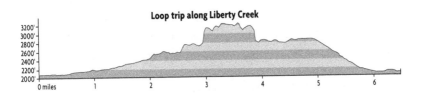

Loop trip along Liberty Creek

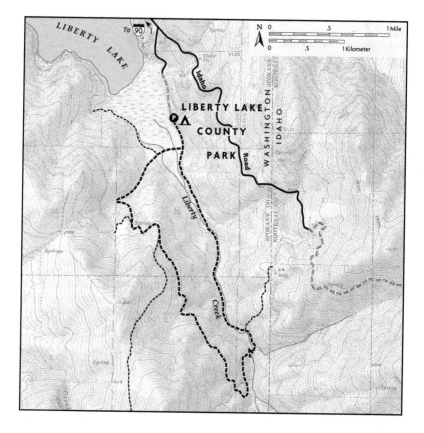

On a recent trip a moose greeted us. Your dog will have plenty of scents to hone in on.

Several miles of trails traverse the park. The recommended hike is a well-marked 6.5-mile loop. If you want more, secondary trails take off from the loop, but they're not as maintained. If you're considering doing them, be sure to take along a good map.

The loop begins on an old road—wide, shaded, nearly level, and a pleasure to walk. Big pines, firs, larches, and cottonwoods line the way. In 0.3 mile you'll come to the loop junction. Take the left trail for an enjoyable ascent along Liberty Creek. The trail climbs 500 feet in 2 miles, always along the creek, crossing it several times on good bridges. There are lots of good places to sit, splash, and enjoy. In spring, blossoming skunk cabbage adds a pungent aroma to the hike.

Opposite: Shawn McHenry and Lida along the Liberty Lake Loop Trail (Photo by Craig Romano)

In 2 miles you'll come to a backcountry camping area in a lovely cedar grove. This 87-acre tract was added to the park in 1993. Beyond the grove, the trail begins to climb steeply. This is a logical turnaround for those desiring an easy hike. To continue the loop, cross the creek and begin the switchback ascent up Sam Hill.

Views of the Liberty Creek valley begin at about 2.5 miles. The forest thins out as the trail continues to climb. In spring, balsamroot and shooting stars paint the trail corridor. In 3 miles you'll come to a pretty waterfall (3000 ft.), a great spot to cool off during the hot summer months.

The trail climbs a little more through cool damp forests and along pretty, tumbling cascades. At 3.5 miles you'll cross the creek for the last time. Soon you'll pass an old cabin site and emerge at Camp Hughes (3250 ft.), a slightly over-used shelter. The loop now utilizes an old road to meander down the ridge, offering plenty of views. It can be hot in the summer, so be sure to carry extra water. After 5.75 miles of hiking you'll emerge in a wildlife-rich wetlands area. Go right at a trail junction, cross Liberty Creek, and return to the loop junction. It's 0.3 mile back to your car from here. The park campground makes for a nice spot to spend the night if the two of you aren't quite ready to leave this natural haven.

43. Cheever Lake–Headquarters Trail

Location: Spokane County
Round Trip: 3 miles
Hiking Time: 2 hours
High Point: 2300 feet
Elevation Gain: 50 feet
Best Hiking Time: March to November
Map: USGS Cheney
Contact: Turnbull National Wildlife Refuge, (509) 235-4723
Notes: Dogs must be leashed. A Refuge Pass or a Golden Eagle Pass is required.

Driving Directions: From Spokane, Washington, take Interstate 90 west to exit 270. Drive 6 miles west on State Route 904 to Cheney. From the downtown traffic light proceed 0.4 mile. Look for a big sign saying "Turnbull National Wildlife Refuge 4 miles." Turn left onto the

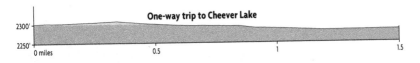

One-way trip to Cheever Lake

Cheney-Plaza Road and drive 4.25 miles. At a big refuge sign, turn left (South Smith Road) and proceed 2 miles to the refuge headquarters. The trail begins opposite the office at the far end of the parking lot.

A bird-watcher's paradise, the Turnbull National Wildlife Refuge is also a nice place for bird dogs. It's also good for dogs not bred for hunting, because the Turnbull is closed to sportsmen, making it an ideal year-round hiking destination. Spring is the best time, with agreeable temperatures, scores of breeding birds, and meadows streaked with flowers. There is a downside to *alla primavera* though: mosquitoes and ticks can be real buggers. Time your visit accordingly.

Although the refuge consists of over 15,000 acres, only 2200 of them are open to the public. This to allow for an undisturbed environment

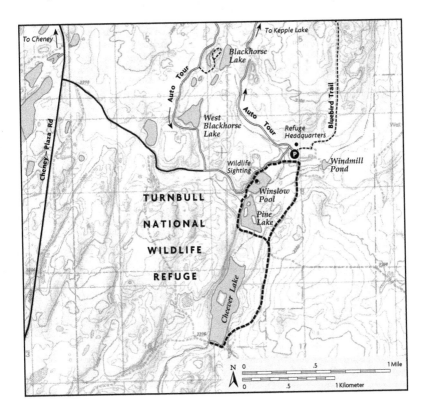

Winslow Pool in the Turnbull National Wildlife Refuge

for the more than 200 species of birds that breed or pass through here. The hike along the Headquarters Trail to Pine and Cheever Lakes is a good representation of the Turnbull Country. This is a land of scab rock and eroded basalt, shallow depressions and scores of lakes. Ponderosa pine forests and bunch and fescue grasslands adorn the lakes and vernal pools.

From the trailhead, follow the Headquarters Trail south. It's a wide and practically flat old road. Except for a few areas of loose gravel the hike is easy and enjoyable. Within minutes you'll approach Headquarters Pond, a small body of water teeming with frogs.

Continue through open countryside. In 0.5 mile you come to a junction. The right goes to Pine Lake, the optional return for this hike or a shorter hike option. Beyond the Pine Lake Trail junction the Headquarters Trail traverses a large grassland. Cheever Lake can be seen to the west. In 1 mile you'll reenter the forest. In 1.5 miles the trail ends at the elongated lake's outlet. If your buddy wants to go for a swim, keep him from disturbing any of the lake's avian residents. They're teeming here. Tell him about the turtles, too.

For a nice variation for the return, swing by Pine Lake. You can hike around Pine or continue back to the refuge headquarters by traveling along the Winslow Pool. It's a 5-minute road walk from the Pine Loop Trailhead to the Headquarters Trailhead. If you and your pup want to explore more, pick up a refuge brochure and check out some of the other trails in the refuge. Consider a return trip in the fall, when the aspens glow golden.

44. Kamiak Butte

Location: The Palouse
Round Trip: 3.5 miles
Hiking Time: 2 hours
High Point: 3641 feet
Elevation Gain: 650 feet
Best Hiking Time: April to November
Map: USGS Albion
Contact: Whitman County Parks, (509) 397-6238
Note: Dogs must be leashed.

Driving Directions: From Colfax, Washington, head east on State Route 272 for 5.5 miles towards the town of Palouse. Bear right on Clear Creek Road and follow it for 8 miles. Make a sharp right-hand turn onto Fugate Road. Proceed 0.75 mile to Kamiak Butte County Park (entrance on left). Alternatively, from Pullman, Washington, travel north on SR 27 for 12 miles. Turn left on Clear Creek Road. Proceed 0.5 mile, bearing left on Fugate Road and continuing another 0.75 mile to the park entrance. Continue on the park road for 0.75 mile to a large parking lot for a picnic area and the trailhead. Water and restrooms are available.

Kamiak Butte offers some of the finest views and best hiking within the entire Palouse. Geologically known as a steptoe (an isolated hill or mountain surrounded by lava flows), 3641-foot Kamiak Butte rises nearly 1000 feet above the rolling loess hills of the Palouse. Although nearby Steptoe Butte may be the more famous of southeastern Washington's natural landmarks, Kamiak is higher and more pristine. With no road to its summit,

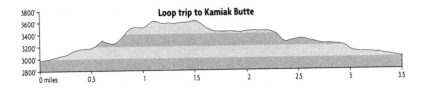

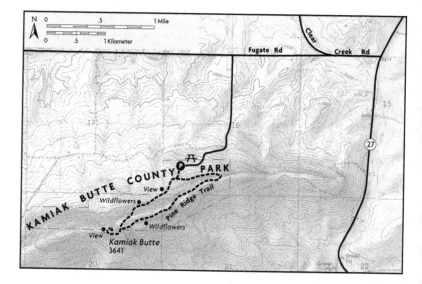

you and your pooch can enjoy Kamiak's extensive views, dazzling wild-flowers, and resident wildlife in relative peace.

A delightful 3.5-mile loop, the Pine Ridge Trail—a designated National Recreation Trail—will take you to the top and along the crest of the butte. Unlike Steptoe Butte to the north, which is completely devoid of trees, Kamiak's northern slope is graced with a mature forest of Douglas fir and ponderosa pine. It may very well be the largest forested tract in all of Whitman County. Best of all, this forest helps protect you from the Palouse's ubiquitous wind and occasional hot sun.

Near an informative kiosk find the trailhead. Immediately you'll come to a junction. The trail to the right (signed to the campground) is the one you'll want to take. You'll be returning via the trail to your left. Proceed west, passing a spur to your right that leads to the park's small campground (yet another good place to base). Soon you'll come to an opening in the forest, an area lush with vegetation and, unfortunately, poison ivy. Keep your dog close. Once you reenter the forest the ivy disappears.

On a somewhat steep route you'll make your way up the butte. The ascent is completely forested, with occasional views to Steptoe Butte and McCroskey Country (Hike 46). It's a well-constructed route with a good surface, but it can get slick in wet weather.

After about 1.5 miles you'll emerge on the crest of the butte and come to a junction. The trail to the right leads 5 minutes to the actual summit of Kamiak (3641 ft.), with good views to the west and south. The loop

continues left, slowly descending along the eastern ridge and undulating between forest and meadows. In spring the wild floral arrangement will mesmerize you. Red, orange, purple, yellow—all colors and shades are represented. Your dog won't care much; he'll be captivated by the myriad of birds and small mammals.

Admire the rolling Palouse countryside as you make your way across the butte. After 1 mile of some of the nicest ridge hiking in all of southeastern Washington, the trail leaves the crest. On a wide path through a series of gentle switchbacks, the loop closes back at the picnic area, where your pooch's tail may indicate that he wants a picnic of his own.

Mittens takes a break beside balsamroot, Kamiak Butte.

45. Indian Cliff

Location: The Palouse
Round Trip: 3 miles
Hiking Time: 2 hours
Round Trip from Hawley's Landing: 5.4 miles
Hiking Time: 3–4 hours
High Point: 2700 feet
Elevation Gain: 500 feet
Maps: USGS Harrison, Chatcolet
Best Hiking Time: April to November
Contact: Heyburn State Park, (208) 686-1308
Notes: Dogs must be leashed. An Idaho State Park Pass is required.

Driving Directions: From Coeur d'Alene, Idaho, take US Highway 95 south for 35 miles to the town of Plummer. Turn left (east) onto State

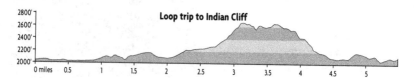

Route 5 and proceed for 6.5 miles. Turn left on Chatcolet Road (signed for Heyburn State Park—Hawley's Landing Campground). If coming from the east, the turnoff is 12 miles from St. Maries. Proceed on Chatcolet Road to the turnoff for Hawley's Landing in 0.25 mile. One mile further, just after passing the paved Trail of the Coeur d'Alenes, a small parking lot on your left indicates the trailhead for the Indian Cliff Trail.

Heyburn State Park consists of over 7800 acres of forest, meadows, and lakes. Established in 1908, it became Idaho's first state park. Protecting land and water where Lake Coeur d'Alene, the St. Joe River, and the Palouse converge, Heyburn offers incredible natural diversity and sublime scenery. And thanks to the hard work of the Civilian Conservation Corps (CCC), Heyburn is graced with family-friendly campgrounds, tranquil picnic grounds, and a good trail system. Heyburn makes for a perfect weekend getaway for you and your pooch, especially in spring and fall when visitation is low.

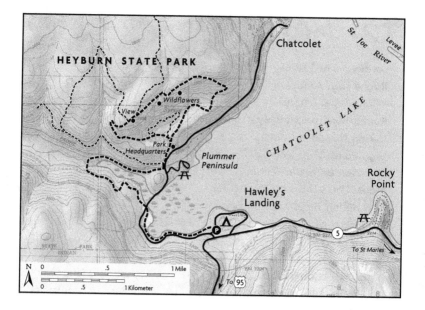

Open pine forest and meadows along the Indian Cliff Trail

The hike up Indian Cliff can be done as a short 3-mile loop or as a longer 5.4-mile lollipop loop from the campground at Hawley's Landing, as suggested here. From the campground find the Lakeshore Trail, which starts across from the registration board. Follow this level and shaded path along Chatcolet Lake for 0.6 mile to the Plummer Point day-use area. Here you can refill your water bottles and scan the marshes for birdlife, which is profuse in this quiet cove.

Now cross Chatcolet Road and follow the Plummer Creek Trail for 0.6 mile. This route takes you a short way up the creek, crosses it on a good bridge, then comes back down on the opposite side, passing by some giant cottonwoods. There are some sections of high grass, so check for ticks. The Plummer Creek Trail ends at the parking lot and trailhead for the Indian Cliff Trail (the beginning for the short hike option).

Proceed for a short ways up the Indian Cliff Trail through an open forest of ponderosa pine to a junction. Take the trail right, signed for

Indian Cliff. You'll be returning to this spot via the trail on the left. Begin climbing on an old logging road. The forest here is full of life, and your dog will probably sense that these woods teem with deer.

After a short level section, the trail switchbacks left and begins to climb the open ridge known as Indian Cliff. For over a mile the two of you will be treated to scenic views and meadows. Indian Cliff offers an exceptional vantage for observing the "river-within-the-lake." When Lake Coeur d'Alene's outlet was dammed, it caused the water level to rise, spilling over and incorporating Round, Benewah, and Chatcolet Lakes into it. All that remains to delineate these lakes is the levee of the St. Joe River, creating the illusion of a river within a lake.

The only thing on this hike that's better than that view is the floral show that's presented each May and June. It rivals Kamiak Butte's. Lupine, balsamroot, syringa, camas, penstemon, stonecrop, and others paint the cliff in a myriad of colors. While you admire the flowers your dog may hone in on some of the reptilian residents of the cliff, such as the rubber boas.

Linger on the ridge for as long as you care, then begin your descent. Through a forest that was burned in 1994, the trail returns to the loop junction. From there, retrace your steps back to the trailhead or campground.

46. Mary Minerva McCroskey Country

Location: The Palouse to Mineral Mountain
Round Trip: 3 miles
Hiking Time: 2 hours
High Point: 4128 feet
Elevation Gain: 400 feet
Korth Trail One-way Trip: 8 miles
Hiking Time: 4 hours
High Point: 3800
Elevation Gain: 700 feet (many ups and downs)
Best Hiking Time: May to October
Map: USGS 7.5 Mission Mountain
Contact: Idaho State Parks and Recreation, (208) 686-1308

Driving Directions: From Coeur d'Alene, Idaho, head south on US Highway 95 for about 60 miles. Just before milepost 371 at the summit

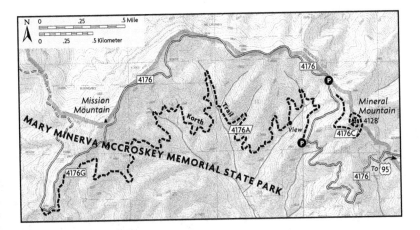

that divides Benewah and Latah counties (along the southern boundary of the Coeur d'Alene Indian Reservation) turn right on a dirt road signed "Skyline Drive" and "Road 4716." Alternatively, from Moscow head north on US 95 for 16 miles. Skyline Drive is just past milepost 371, 1 mile beyond the highway rest area. Take Skyline Drive 0.5 mile to the state park boundary and information kiosk. Korth Trail is 3.25 miles further. For Mineral Mountain continue 1 mile more to a road junction signed "Mineral Mountain 4760." Park here on the side of the road.

One of Idaho's least known state parks, 5000-acre-plus McCroskey is also one of the Gem State's largest parks. A gift to the state in 1955 from Virgil Talmage McCroskey, as a tribute to his mother and all pioneer women of the Northwest, McCroskey State Park has changed little in fifty years.

The park occupies a long ridge that ranges in elevation from 3000 to 4200 feet. It marks the transition zone between the grasslands of the Palouse and the rich forests of the Panhandle Mountain ranges. Open

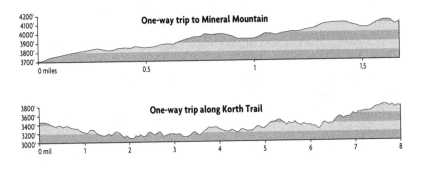

View across Mary Minerva McCroskey region from Korth Trail

ponderosa forests flank the park's western reaches, while damp stands of cedar and grand fir blanket the park's eastern lands. Seven different ecological zones can be found in McCroskey, supporting a diverse array of wildlife including moose, coyote, elk, and black bear.

McCroskey offers miles of lonely walking in a rich natural area. But before you and your intrepid buddy venture this way it should be noted that McCroskey's trails are actually old roads—and they're open for multiple-use. Does that mean you'll be yielding to horse, mountain bikes, and motorcycles? Not necessarily, for although these uses are allowed, there is very little use in this park off Skyline Drive. The Korth Trail has patches of moss and grass growing on it, a far cry from the deep ruts of other multi-use trails. So go out and explore the park, but be aware that you may encounter users of other means.

Your two best bets for walking in McCroskey are the Korth Trail (sometimes referred to as the Old Corinth Road) and Mineral Mountain. The Korth Trail is an old road that hugs the ridgeline below the crest for over 8 miles. It traverses cedar dens, open pine forests, grassy slopes with views, and quiet cool ravines. Elevation change is minimal and the grade is always gentle. There's water along the way, but by late summer many of the creeks run dry. Moose are common along the trail and chances for encountering other big beasties are good as well.

The road-trail up to Mineral Mountain is a real treat. The old road snakes for 1.5 miles around the mountain a couple of times before attaining the 4128-foot summit. There was once a fire lookout here, and you'll soon realize why. The views from this unimposing peak are incredible, from Lake Coeur D'Alene in the north to Steptoe and Kamiak Buttes rising above the Palouse hills in the west, to Moscow Mountain in the south.

In late spring Mineral is awash in brilliant colors of blossoming wildflowers. Copious larkspur transforms Mineral into a purple mountain majesty. Balsamroot add a golden touch. The summit of the peak is broad and grassy.

If you're considering spending a night in McCroskey Country, there is a quiet, primitive campground complete with a large picnic shelter 1.75 miles from the Mineral Mountain Trail. There's no water, however, so be sure to pack some in.

IDAHO SELKIRKS

47. Priest Lake–Lakeshore Trail

Location: Selkirk Mountains
One-way Trip: 7.6 miles
Hiking Time: 4 hours
High Point: 2600 feet
Elevation Gain: 200 feet
Maps: USGS Priest Lake NE, Priest Lake NW
Best Hiking Time: May to November
Contact: Idaho Panhandle National Forests, Priest Lake Ranger District, (208) 443-2512

Driving Directions: From the town of Priest River, Idaho, head north on State Route 57 for 36 miles to Nordman. Turn right on the paved road that heads to Reeder Bay. Follow this road, which becomes Forest Road 2512, for 4.5 miles to the south trailhead. The north trailhead is 7.25 miles further at the Beaver Creek Campground.

If you're looking for an easy hike for ol' Rover, one that's perfect for both warm sunny days and cool rainy ones, look no farther than the Lakeshore Trail. This national recreation trail travels for more than 7 miles along the pristine northwestern shoreline of Priest Lake, the prettiest and most remote of northern Idaho's grand lakes.

One-way trip to Bottle Bay

A nearly level path that leads to secluded beaches, coves, and cozy lakeside campgrounds, the Lakeshore National Recreation Trail can be accessed from four points, all originating off FR 2512. As you might expect from such an easily accessible trail, this hike is quite popular, especially with mountain bikers and trail runners. However, if you come here early or late in the season—when the youngsters are in school, the boats are in mooring, and the songbirds are in Mexico—chances are that you and your furry friend will have the trail to yourselves. Even during the heat of summer, trail use can be fairly light, when many would-be users are sunbathing instead. In any case, it's best to keep your buddy on a leash.

The description given here is from south to north, but any direction you travel on this trail offers beautiful lakeside hiking. The trail begins in a cool hemlock grove, passes the ruins of an old cabin, and soon emerges along Priest Lake. Good views of the tiny Twin Islands and of Chimney Rock in the Selkirk Crest come into focus. Look for ospreys, eagles, and loons. After 1.5 miles the first of many wonderful sandy beaches is reached. This one is ringed by giant western white pines. This increasingly rare conifer is common along this trail.

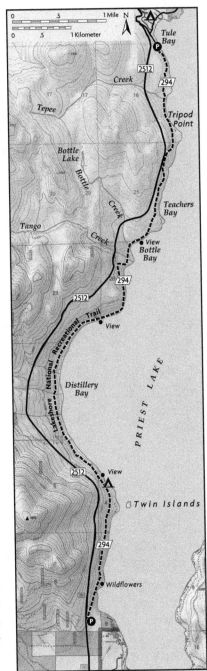

Mittens at beach along Lakeshore Trail

The next mile takes you through a forest of even bigger trees, pines as well as cedars. Watch for moose—they're quite common here. Bear frequent the lakeshore as well. Your pup has probably already honed in on some nice "trail apples." After 2.5 miles you'll come to the first of several creeks (all bridged) along this lovely path. Soon afterwards you'll reach a signed junction. The left goes to FR 2512; continue right. In 3.5 miles the trail skirts along Distillery Bay (look for whiskey jacks also known as gray jays), revealing a series of gorgeous beaches. In 4.5 miles another spur heads left to the road; keep right. Within 0.25 mile you'll come to Bottle Bay (product of the distillery perhaps?). Here you'll find nearly a dozen campsites, a privy, and a sprawling beach ringing the cove. This is a great spot to overnight, picnic, or swim. Your dog has probably already chosen the latter. Join her!

Bottle Bay makes a nice turnaround if you don't care to go any further. If you've arranged for a shuttle or plan to do a 15.2-mile round trip, proceed another 2.5 miles to the trail's northern terminus at the Beaver Creek Campground. Expect more beaches, campsites, big trees, and good hiking.

48. Upper Priest River

Location: Selkirk Mountains
Round Trip: 16 miles
Hiking Time: 8 hours
High Point: 3400 feet
Elevation Gain: 650 feet
Map: USGS Continental Mountain
Best Hiking Time: June to November
Contact: Idaho Panhandle National Forests, Priest Lake Ranger District, (208) 443-2512

Driving Directions: From the town of Priest River, Idaho, head north on State Route 57 for 36 miles to Nordman. Continue north on Forest Road 302 until the pavement ends in 4 miles. After 10 miles, pass the Stagger Inn Campground. In 15 miles reach Granite Pass and a four-way junction. Proceed north on FR 1013 for 11 miles. The trailhead is on the left before the road makes a switchback and begins to climb.

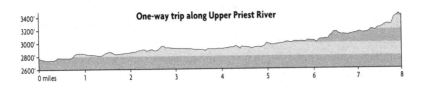

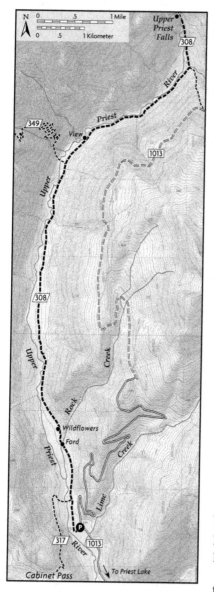

The upper reaches of the Priest River contain some of the finest old-growth forest remaining within the entire Selkirk Range. Giant western red cedars line the pristine waterway. Big hemlocks, too. Yew, devil's club, and maidenhair fern permeate the understory. The dark, damp primeval forest of the Upper Priest rivals any ancient forest of the Cascades. This is truly a special place that deserves to be added to the adjacent Salmo-Priest Wilderness.

Big trees aren't the only stakeholders in this ecosystem: Grizzlies and woodland caribou need this forest, too. As for you and your furry pal, your wayward spirits need the Upper Priest as well. It is a redeeming landscape, a sacred place, and a refuge where the two of you can easily while away the hours.

Visit the Upper Priest on a misty day. The thick forest canopy will shelter you. Or visit it on a steamy hot day when the green shroud traps the cool moist breezes from the river. No need to pack much water on this trip, for plenty of it flows the entire way.

The trail immediately enters the cathedral forest, but the Priest is not nearby. Along a soft carpet of needles, the trail works its way up the gentle valley. In 0.5 mile you'll come to Rock Creek. In high water prepare for wet feet. Lots of creek crossings are yet to come. Some are bridged, some are not—your dog could probably care less either way. Look for fresh beaver activity.

Craig Romano at American Falls (Upper Priest Falls)

In about 1.5 miles the river appears. The trail will hug it dearly for the remainder of the hike. Lunch spots, play spots, rest spots, and camping spots are plentiful along the Priest. Although your dog will no doubt enjoy all of the running water, you'll probably be most amazed by the giant cedars.

After 5 miles you'll come to the junction with Trail 349, which travels to Little Snowy Top via an unrelenting climb. Stay in the valley; Snowy Top is more easily reached via the Shedroof Divide (Hike 33). Further up the river, good campsites abound if the two of you decide to spend the night. After 7.5 miles you'll come to a junction. To the right, Continental Trail 28 climbs steeply for 2.3 miles back to FR 1013. Instead, take the left trail for a 0.5-mile hike to Upper Priest Falls. Although this is a nice spot to play and soak, camping here is marginal. Return to one of those prime spots you saw on the way in, or enjoy the full hike out, visiting all of those giant trees again.

49. Pyramid and Ball Lakes

Location: Selkirk Mountains
Round Trip: 4 miles
Hiking Time: 3 hours
High Point: 6708 feet
Elevation Gain: 1300 feet
Map: USGS Pyramid Peak
Best Hiking Time: July to mid-October
Contact: Idaho Panhandle National Forests, Bonners Ferry Ranger District, (208) 267-5561

Driving Directions: To reach the trailhead, from Bonners Ferry, Idaho, take the city center exit off US Highway 2/95. Follow Riverside Street west to the Kootenai National Wildlife Refuge. After about 5 miles bear right on the West Side Road passing the refuge headquarters. Ten miles beyond the refuge headquarters turn left onto Forest Road 634 (Trout Creek). Follow FR 634 west for 9 miles to the trailhead. Parking is limited and is prohibited on the road. If there are no spaces available, consider an alternative hike nearby such as Snow Lake (Hike 51) or West Fork Lake (Hike 50).

Although the Selkirks have certainly seen an increase in visitors over the years, these mountains remain wild. A handful of grizzly bears roam the crest, and the last herd of caribou south of the Canadian border call this range home. The presence of grizzlies may be of concern to you and your dog. However, you are more of a threat to the grizzlies than they are to you. Grizzly sightings are rare. Keep your canine companion under strict control. With care, there's still plenty of room to roam for you, your dog, and all the wild critters in this special corner of Idaho.

The rocky and jagged Selkirks are blessed with an abundance of alpine lakes. Some, like the Roman Nose Lakes, have become quite popular. Pyramid and the Ball Lakes are certainly not secrets, but if you visit them during

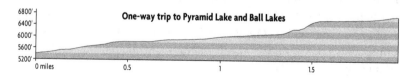

One-way trip to Pyramid Lake and Ball Lakes

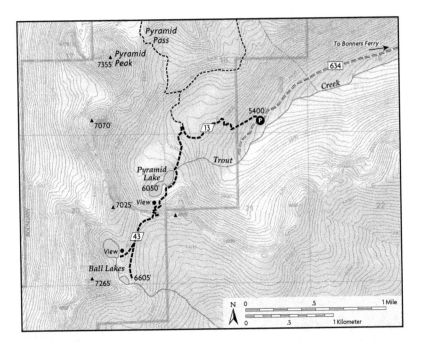

the week it's still possible to have them to yourself. Three prime gems, all within 2 miles. Most hikers, however, stop only at the Pyramid. The Ball Lakes require a little more effort and offer a lot more solitude.

From an elevation of 5420 feet, Trail 13 begins in an old cut but quickly transitions into a mature forest of fir and spruce. In 0.5 mile you'll come to a signed trail junction. Take the path left, signed "Pyramid Lake Trail 43." It's an easy hike to the lake through a fairyland landscape of babbling brooks and giant boulders. In 1 mile you'll reach Pyramid Lake (6050 ft.). It's shallow and filled with reeds, but your dog won't mind. Flat boulders for sitting and sunning are on hand if you don't care to join your buddy for a splash.

Don't get too comfortable here, for the Ball lakes are more enticing. Cross Pyramid's outlet on a good bridge and continue further on Trail 13. Over ledges and through heather meadows the trail climbs 700 feet in the next mile, providing great views over Pyramid Lake and an occasional glimpse of the deeply cut Trout Creek valley. There are lots of huckleberry bushes along the way—be wary of bears.

Two miles from the start, the trail delivers the two of you to a junction. To the right is Upper Ball Lake, a cool, deep body of water jumping with fish. Big shoreline rocks are prime spots for contemplation. To the

Pyramid Lake with granite boulders characteristic of Selkirk Mountain Range

left is Lower Ball Lake. Tucked out of view, the lower lake has a few nice and protected campsites. The open country around the lake may look enticing for further explorations, but for your four-legged friend it may be a bit rugged. Instead, she may want to hang out and play what the lake's namesake suggests—ball! This is a great place to fetch and splash and enjoy the Selkirk backcountry.

50. West Fork Lake and Mountain

Location: Selkirk Mountains
Round Trip: 10 miles
Hiking Time: 6–7 hours
High Point: 6416 feet
Elevation Gain: 2300 feet
Maps: USGS Smith Peak, Shorty Peak, Caribou Creek
Best Hiking Time: mid-June to mid-October
Contact: Idaho Panhandle National Forests, Bonners Ferry Ranger District, (208) 267-5561

Driving Directions: From Bonners Ferry, Idaho, follow US Highway 95 north for 15 miles to State Route 1. Follow SR 1 for 1 mile. Turn left on County Road 45, signed "Copeland Bridge." In 3.5 miles (after crossing the Kootenai River) turn right (north) at a junction on to the Westside Road. Proceed 9 miles. The road makes a sharp left (west) and becomes Forest Road 281 (Smith Creek). In 6 miles the pavement ends. In 7.6 miles from the sharp turn, bear left at a junction to cross Smith Creek. In 3.3 more miles come to a second junction; bear right onto FR 2446. In 1 mile FR 2446 ends at the trailhead, with parking for about five vehicles.

This hike will take you to one of the largest lakes and one of the prettiest summits in the Selkirk Range. A wonderful destination throughout the hiking season, with cool old-growth forests and refreshing creeks, it's especially nice when the Kootenai River valley is frying below. Of course plenty of moisture means plenty of mosquitoes. Remember, too, that you're in grizzly country, so stay bear-aware. It's unlikely you'll see one, but the bears ensure that this area is a true wilderness even if it hasn't yet been federally designated.

Trail 21 begins in an old cut. Utilizing a former logging road—now fully converted to trail—the route begins gently. It may be hot, for there is little

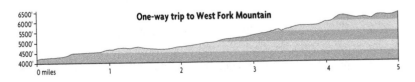

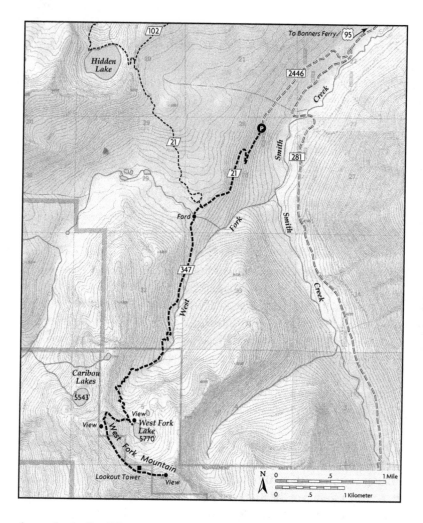

forest shade. You'll have good views looking down the Smith Creek valley.

After an easy 1.5 miles you and Spot will enter mature forest and come to a junction with Trail 347 (4550 ft). Trail 21 continues right to a wonderful backcountry cabin before climbing 1200 feet on its way to Hidden Lake (a worthy hike in itself). Your destination, however, is West Fork Lake, so turn left at the junction and follow Trail 347.

You'll immediately cross a lovely creek. Your pooch may want to rehydrate, and from here to the lake there's no shortage of water. The trail makes its way through some old and huge western cedars, and around the stumps of less fortunate specimens. In about 3 miles you'll begin to climb a series of gentle switchbacks. Meadows and bogs grace the thinning forest. In 4 miles the climb eases and you'll come to a junction (5770 ft.). West Fork Lake is to the left, the mountain is to the right.

It's a mere 3-minute walk from the junction to the lake. The large body of water is shallow, guaranteeing a warm splash by late summer. The shoreline is grassy and can be a bit boggy, but there are plenty of large rocks to plop down on. Campsites might be a tad damp, but there are a

West Fork Lake with views toward West Fork Mountain

handful of decent ones. Lots of moose and bear tracks may suggest you won't be alone. From the lake's outlet you're granted a wonderful view of West Fork Mountain, guarding the southern flanks.

If the sight of the peak entices you, it's a good little climb from the lake. Most dogs shouldn't have too much difficulty either. The route traverses open ledges, however, so keep your pal nearby. From the lake, it's about a 1 mile and 600-foot climb to the 6416-foot summit. Your dog will pant from the climb, while you'll drool over the views. Gaze out at a sea of peaks that encompass three states and British Columbia. From the Salmo-Priest country to the rugged Selkirk Crest, it's a strikingly beautiful landscape. West Fork Lake twinkles below, perhaps enticing your buddy for one more dip before heading back to the car.

51. Snow Lake

Location: Selkirk Mountains
Round Trip: 9.5 miles
Hiking Time: 6 hours
High Point: 6000 feet
Elevation Gain: 1600 feet
Map: USGS Roman Nose
Best Hiking Time: July to mid-October
Contact: Idaho Panhandle National Forests, Bonners Ferry Ranger District, (208) 267-5561

Driving Directions: From Sandpoint, Idaho, drive north on US Highway 2/95, turning left (west) into the village of Naples. Bear right on Deep Creek Road. Follow it for 5.7 miles, then turn left on West Side Road (County Road 13), signed "Snow Creek Road 402 2 miles." Follow it for 2.1 miles, coming to a Y-junction. Turn left on Forest Road 402 and follow it for 9.5 miles to the trailhead, located at the junction with Cooks Pass Road (FR 661). Park on the left road shoulder. Trail 185 begins as an old road.

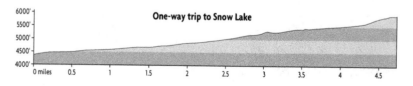

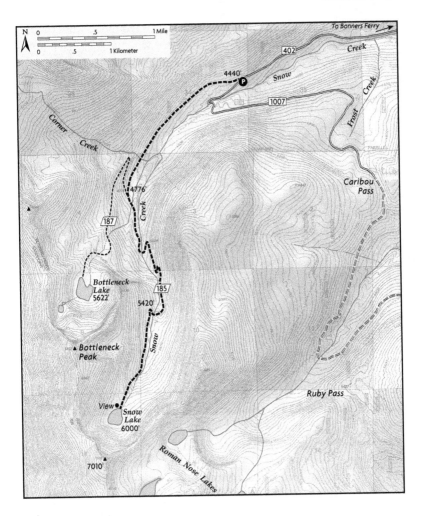

Finding a quiet lake in the Idaho Selkirks can be as difficult as spotting the resident woodland caribou herd. Why? Many of these alpine gems are easily accessible, thanks to decades of logging roads punching farther into the backcountry. Even some of the more remote lakes see healthy numbers of hikers—the word's out on these spectacular wilderness lakes.

Snow Lake was once an easy hike, a mere 3-mile round trip. But the surrounding forest paid a price; the road to the trail was used for logging the valley. Once the big trees were hauled away, the road was abandoned. Before you fret about the loss of an easy hike, consider this: The road

Sailor along the Snow Lake Trail

has been reverted to trail, the forest is growing back, and wildlife is returning. Snow Lake is slowly sinking back into wilderness. A longer hike means fewer people. You and your dog may have the chance to experience a high-country Selkirk Lake alone.

Trail 185 may resemble a road at its start, but it's officially a trail now. You won't see tire marks in the mud, only deer and bear tracks. The resident snowshoe hares will drive your hound crazy, too, so keep a good grip on him!

In 0.25 mile you'll reach a creek crossing. There are plenty more along the way—water is bountiful on this trail. Snow Creek is never out of sight or sound. In 1.75 miles you'll come to a junction (4776 ft.). Trail 187 heads right 1.75 miles to Bottleneck Lake, and chances are if you've encountered anyone else on this hike, that's where they're going.

The way to Snow Lake continues left. There are some open areas to traverse and they can be hot in midday. Think Snow (Lake)! In 2.5 miles the trail crosses Snow Creek, a delight in summer but a fright in spring. Through a series of long switchbacks through the old cuts, the trail makes its way higher. At 3.5 miles a second crossing of Snow Creek is required. Lots of sunny creekside ledges may tempt you and Rover to stop, but don't yet—the lake is just over a mile away.

However, it's a steep mile. There are plenty of huckleberries to feast on, so watch for bears. Once the climbing commences you'll enter a boggy area where you may see moose. At 4.75 miles the quiet waters of Snow Lake (6000 ft.) greet you. The lake is shallow but its waters remain cool because the slopes above sport snowfields into August.

Much of Snow Lake is surrounded by scree, bog, or forest, making camping less than ideal. Prospects for lakeshore exploration are good. The open slopes to the north invite wandering, too. Resident larches make Snow Lake a beautiful destination in the fall.

52. Deep Creek–Kootenai National Wildlife Refuge

Location: Selkirk Mountains
Round Trip: 4.4 miles
Hiking Time: 2–3 hours
High Point: 1700 feet
Elevation Gain: 10 feet
Maps: Kootenai National Wildlife Refuge, U.S. Fish and Wildlife Service
Best Hiking Time: late March through November, except for hunting season
Contact: Kootenai National Wildlife Refuge, Bonners Ferry, Idaho, (208) 267-3888
Note: Dogs must be leashed from April 1 through August 15.

Driving Directions: From Sandpoint, Idaho, travel north on US Highway 2/95 to Bonners Ferry. Take Riverside Street exit and head west, following signs for Kootenai National Wildlife Refuge. In 4 miles enter the refuge, which is marked by a big sign. Turn right into a large trailhead.

The Kootenai National Wildlife Refuge is a great destination for well-behaved and inquisitive dogs. The 2774-acre reserve was established in 1965 to protect habitat for migratory waterfowl. Over 200 species of birds nest or pass through the refuge annually, including teals, grebes, harriers, snipes, terns, vireos, and meadowlarks. The refuge consists primarily of wetlands, meadows, and riparian forests, at the base of the Selkirk Mountains on the Kootenai River. It's a great place for an early-season hike or a lazy summer-afternoon saunter.

Leash restrictions apply primarily during the breeding season. In fall they're lifted, mainly for the benefit of retrievers used for hunting.

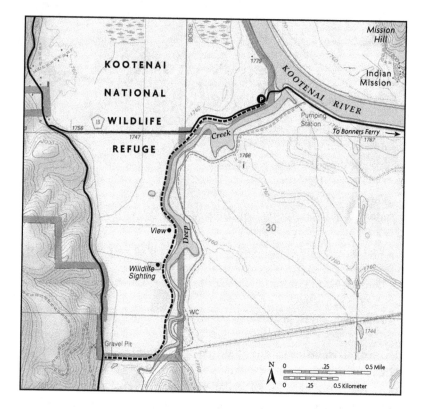

Non-hunting hikers and dogs will want to shy away from the refuge during hunting season. Consult the refuge headquarters for season dates.

Before you begin your hike, be sure to check out the trailhead kiosk and grab a map and brochure. Your dog, of course, isn't interested in any of this; she just wants to start sniffing around. The trail starts across the road from the parking lot on a dike along Deep Creek, a tributary of the Kootenai.

The climb to the dike, all 10 feet or so, is the only climb the two of you will have to make. Mosey down the wide trail and let nature tease your senses and soothe your souls. Cottonwoods line the trail, filling the air with a pungent aroma and the trail with a snowlike cottony blanket.

Kootenai's main appeal is its wildlife viewing; however, the scenery is also quite appealing. Take time to admire the large valley, to appreciate the reflections of big white puffy clouds in the placid slough and pond waters, and to watch ospreys rippling those waters as they plunge for fish. In springtime, birdsong fills the air along the Deep Creek Trail.

Kootenai National Wildlife Refuge

Your dog may not notice all of the avian activity, but the flurry of grasshopper commotion on the ground will keep her alert and nipping.

In 1.25 miles there are good overlooks of heron and teal ponds. The trail continues along Deep Creek, now lined with hawthorns and dogwood. Lots of thistles, too. In 1.75 miles the trail turns westward away from the creek and skirts the southern shore of South Pond. In 2.2 miles the trail ends at Westside Road in a quiet stand of ponderosa pine. Turn around and enjoy the hike all over again. You have more birds to see and your best friend has more vegetation to sniff.

COEUR D'ALENE RIVER

53. Upper Coeur d'Alene River

Location: Coeur d'Alene River
Round Trip: 11.4 miles
Hiking Time: 6–7 hours
High Point: 3200 feet
Elevation Gain: 400 feet
Maps: USGS Cathedral Peak, Jordan Creek
Best Hiking Time: May to November
Contact: Idaho Panhandle National Forests, Coeur d'Alene River
Ranger District, (208) 664-2318

Driving Directions: From Coeur d'Alene, Idaho, head east on Interstate 90 to Kingston exit 43. Proceed east on paved Forest Road 9 for 21 miles to the settlement of Prichard. Continue straight (north) on paved FR 208. FR 9 turns right (east) and heads to Thompson Pass. On FR 208 continue for 26 miles. Just before a bridge crossing the Coeur d'Alene you'll find a paved pull-out and the trailhead for Coeur d'Alene River Trail 20.

Locals have long referred to the upper reaches of the Coeur d'Alene River as the North Fork of the Coeur d'Alene (although there was already a

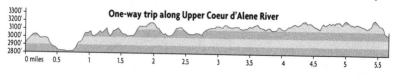

One-way trip along Upper Coeur d'Alene River

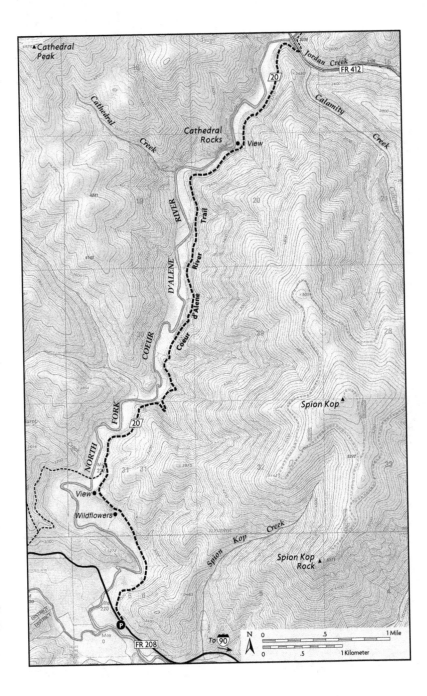

Upper Coeur d'Alene River canyon

branch named such). This could cause some confusion to those who don't know this river so well. Nevertheless, the locals' reference is sticking. The latest Forest Service map honors the name North Fork for this section of the upper Coeur d'Alene. And as far as the real North Fork, that's now the Little North Fork. Confused? None of this, of course, matters to your dog. Whatever *you* decide to call this stretch of river it'll probably include the adjectives "beautiful" and "pristine"—unlike the South Fork, which has been poisoned with a century's worth of mining wastes.

Coeur d'Alene River Trail 20 is a well-constructed, well-maintained trail that parallels the roadless upper reaches of the river—14 miles of wild waterway. Forest Road 412 (accessed from FR 208 17.5 miles south of trailhead) dissects the trail in two, making it possible to do this hike one-way if a shuttle can be arranged. What's described here is the southern section of trail. The northern section is also a fine hike but it requires driving rough access roads and may involve some tricky creek crossings. The southern trail section can be hiked by all breeds of hikers and dogs—and it's easily accessible.

The only downside to this stretch of trail is that for all the time it runs along the river, it's actually only near it in a few places. Most of the time you are on a bluff high above it—but what a bluff! The views of the river canyon are breathtaking. And even though the trail makes little contact with the river, there's no shortage of water because many small creeks are crossed.

Begin by climbing up a warm hillside. Shade comes soon enough. In 0.5 mile the trail drops to a marshy meadow close to the river. Look for moose. (Mittens saw her first one here. "Now *that* is a big dog!" she was thinking.) Enjoy some level walking, then begin climbing to a bluff overlooking a bend in the river. Keep your dog close by, for it's a precipitous drop on the other side. Continue climbing and at 2.25 miles the way eases up. It's now a relaxing hike through forest, along open slopes, and across creek gullies. At about 4.5 miles you'll be able to get a good glimpse across the river to the hoodoos that form Cathedral Rocks. At 5.7 miles you'll come to the end of this segment of trail after crossing rushing Jordan Creek on a good bridge. If the Coeur d'Alene has been teasing you with its inaccessibility, the Jordan will make up for it. Just don't spook the American dippers on your way to its banks.

From here you have several choices: Return and enjoy the trail all over again, spend the night at Jordan Camp just across the bridge over the Coeur d'Alene (river access), or continue another 8 miles on the northern section of trail.

54. Marie Creek

Location: Coeur d'Alene River
Round Trip: 10 miles
Hiking Time: 5 hours
High Point: 2900 feet
Elevation Gain: 550 feet
Map: USGS Wolf Lodge
Best Hiking Time: April to November
Contact: Idaho Panhandle National Forests, Coeur d'Alene River Ranger District, (208) 664-2318

Driving Directions: From Coeur d'Alene, Idaho, travel east on Interstate 90 to exit 22, signed for Harrison and the Wolf Lodge District. Turn left (north), cross the interstate, then turn right (east) onto Wolf Lodge Road. Just shy of a mile you will make a left (north) turn onto

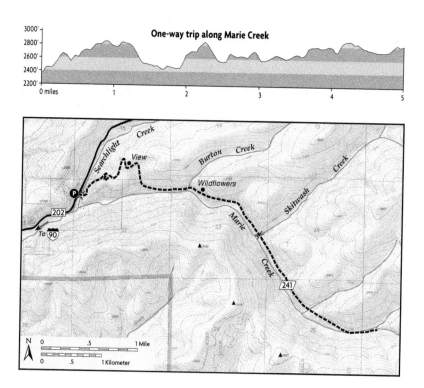

Footbridge over creek to Marie Creek Trailhead

Wolf Lodge Creek Road. Follow Wolf Lodge Creek Road for 3.5 miles (making sure to bear left at a confusing intersection at 1.75 miles). Now make a right-hand turn (east) onto Marie Creek Road (Forest Road 202) and proceed for 1.25 miles, turning right on a dirt road. This road leads 0.1 mile to a large parking area, the trailhead for the Marie Creek Trail.

The Marie Creek Trail offers a great leg-stretcher just 10 miles from downtown Coeur d'Alene. Nothing particularly stunning here, just miles of quiet trail along a tranquil little creek. There are some big trees scattered about and in early season lots of wildflowers. But the best thing about this trail aside from its proximity to the city is that it is completely motor- and wheel-free. In the Coeur d'Alene National Forest, that's a rarity.

Primarily used by equestrians, the trail sees a fair amount of two-legged visitors as well. However, this trail isn't heavily visited, so you and your dog shouldn't have many encounters with others.

Begin by crossing Searchlight Creek. Hikers use the bridge; dogs do as you please. Next, the trail sets out to climb a small ridge. The tread is good and the grade of the switchbacks easy. In 0.75 mile you'll crest the ridge and begin a descent into the Marie Creek valley. In 1.5 miles the trail makes contact with the creek at a nice grassy spot, perfect for a picnic.

It's now a pretty level hike through pine forests, cedar groves, and flower-laden meadows. Continue up the valley, cross Burton Creek (bridged), and after 3 miles reach Skitwash Creek (bridged) and a trail junction. It's possible to take the left-hand trail up Skitwish Creek for a 6-mile return to the trailhead, but it's not recommended. After following Skitwish for 0.5 mile this trail leaves the valley and gains some serious elevation over dry and monotonous terrain. The trail, however, is in good shape if you want the exercise.

Another option is to continue up Marie Creek for another 2 miles where the trail eventually ends near a tributary. As you listen to the creek's flowing water and the chatter of the resident nuthatches, thrushes, and woodpeckers, you'll have to remind yourself that you're less than 15 miles from the hubbub of Coeur d'Alene.

ST. JOE COUNTRY

55. Simmons Creek

Location: St. Joe River Country
Round Trip: 5 miles
Hiking Time: 3 hours
High Point: 3800 feet
Elevation Gain: 400 feet
Map: USGS Red Ives Peak
Best Hiking Time: late May through October
Contact: Idaho Panhandle National Forests (St. Joe), Avery Ranger
  District, (208) 245-4517

Driving Directions: From St. Maries, Idaho, follow the St. Joe River Road (Forest Road 50) east towards Avery. Beyond Avery, and after 75 long but scenic miles, come to a junction with FR 218. Bear right on FR 218 and proceed for 1.4 miles. Just beyond the Gold Creek Campground and before the bridge over Simmons Creek turn left on a short spur road, which ends at a large clearing in 0.25 mile. Trail 80 begins at the east end of the clearing. This trail can also be accessed from St. Regis, Montana, by following the Little Joe Road (FR 282, which becomes paved FR 50 in Idaho) for 29 miles to the junction with FR 218.

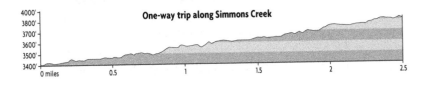

One-way trip along Simmons Creek

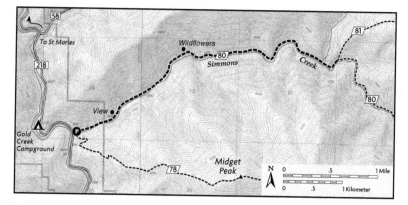

The upper St. Joe country contains dozens of quiet valleys ripe for you and your pooch to explore. Trails traverse nearly every one of them, hugging these wild and roaring tributaries of the mighty St. Joe River. Unfortunately, many of these trails are neglected. A lack of funds and, in some cases, interest often makes these byways a challenge to follow. However, there's a handful that are still quite passable. The Simmons Creek Trail is one of them. Whatever comfort you give up along this route, you'll be rewarded with solitude, which rarely exists on the nearby and well-maintained St. Joe River Trail.

Simmons Creek Trail 80 begins behind a sometimes-active conservation camp. If the troops are in, this will most likely be your last interaction with fellow humans and dogs before heading up the wild valley. The first mile of trail is in decent shape. Although the trail never ventures away from the creek, often running right up alongside it, the valley can still get quite warm. Old burns and talus slopes have to be traversed, and in the summer they can get hot; however, ample rain in this area minimizes the frequency of extreme temperatures.

In 1 mile the valley opens up, providing good views upstream. Enjoy watching the frothing creek. Scan the open hillsides for deer, bear, and elk. Your pooch may already have spotted one. Continue along. Hanging cliffs above the trail warrant some snooping around as well.

The trail improves as you enter a forest of mature lodgepole pine. In 2.5 miles you'll come to the North Fork of Simmons Creek. This is a good turnaround, especially if the North Fork is roaring. You can check out a fish gauging station, watch the dippers, and look at the hawks above. If the brushy trail hasn't tired the two of you out—and if the creek's ford looks safe—continue up the valley. The trail carries on for more than 10 miles.

Simmons Creek

56. Upper St. Joe River

Location: St. Joe River Country
One-way Trip: 17 miles
Hiking Time: 2 days
High Point: 4690 feet
Elevation Gain: 890 feet
Round Trip to Bacon Creek: 14 miles
Hiking Time: 7 hours
High Point: 4050 feet
Elevation Gain: 400 feet
Maps: USGS Bacon Peak, Simmons Peak, Illinois Peak
Best Hiking Time: late May through October
Contact: Idaho Panhandle National Forests (St. Joe), Avery Ranger District, (208) 245-4517

Driving Directions: From St. Maries, Idaho, follow the St. Joe River Road (Forest Road 50) east towards Avery. Beyond Avery, and after 75 long but scenic miles, come to a junction with FR 218. Bear right on FR 218 and follow it 11 miles to its end at the Spruce Creek Campground. Trail 48 begins from the far end of the campground. This trail can also be accessed from St. Regis, Montana, by following the Little Joe Road (FR 282, which becomes paved FR 50 in Idaho) for 29 miles to the junction with FR 218.

The St. Joe is one of the prettiest rivers in all of northern Idaho. Classified as a National Wild and Recreation River, it has been afforded much protection. Although most of its course is paralleled by roads, a 17-mile section in its upper reaches is pure wilderness. Here, a well-maintained trail travels along this lifeline of the Bitterroot Mountains far from roads and human activity. It is a popular trail though, and on a summer weekend scores of hikers, anglers, and equestrians take to it. However, as you venture further up the St. Joe, the numbers diminish and the chances

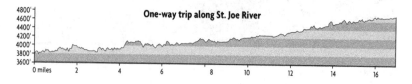

One-way trip along St. Joe River

Mittens along Upper St. Joe River

increase that you'll meet the residents—the bear, deer, and elk—that live in this wild corner of the Gem State.

The St. Joe River Trail can usually be hiked by May, but there may be a few tough creek crossings. During a wet spring, wait until June before venturing up the valley. The first 5 miles of trail are popular with equestrians en route to a private lodge, so it's best to have your buddy leashed.

It's a pretty straightforward hike. Go as far as the two of you would like. Even if you're intent on doing the 17 miles in its entirety, many inviting campsites, quiet groves, and scenic bluffs will entice you to stay awhile. The trail never ventures far from the river. Begin in a cool forest of spruce and fir. Two creek crossings must be navigated within the first 0.5 mile. In 1 mile, come to a junction with the Elbow Ridge Trail, one

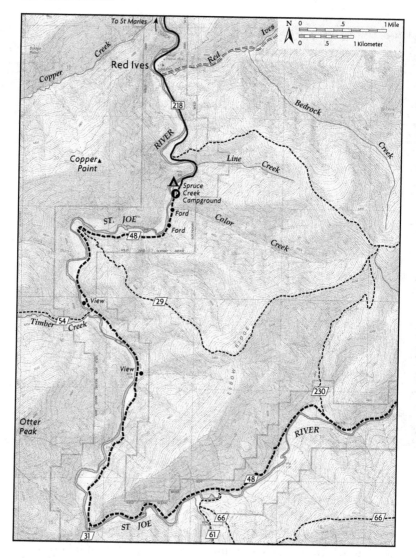

of many trails that radiate from the valley. Pause to take in a great view of the tumbling river.

In 2.5 miles you'll come to Timber Creek and yet another trail junction. Just beyond is a lovely riverside campsite, complete with view. Continue up the valley. A few short climbs slow you down, if the scenery hasn't. Your dog is probably going crazy by now, picking up scents from all of the game trails.

At 5 miles comes the junction to the St. Joe Lodge. Trail use decreases

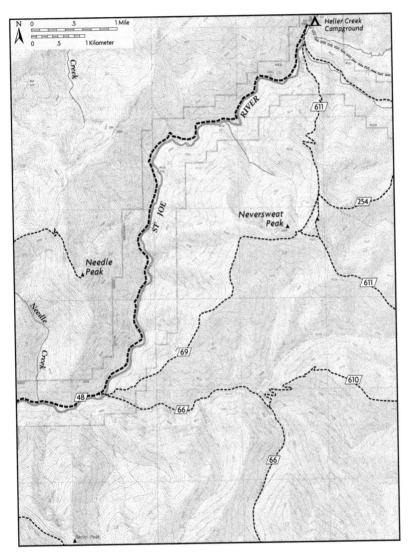

from this point, while chances for seeing bear and elk increase. In 5.5 miles you'll come to the junction with the My Creek Trail and more good campsites. At 6 miles you'll find a charming spot along the river, with prime camping spots. At 7 miles you'll cross the Bacon Loop Trail, a good turnaround for day hikers. If you and your pup are intent on going all the way to Heller Creek, however, you're pretty much in for more of the same—incredible backcountry in one of the most wildlife-enriched valleys in the Inland Northwest.

57. Mallard Lake and Peak

Location: St. Joe River Country
Round Trip to Lake: 10.5 miles
Hiking Time: 4–5 hours
High Point: 6100 feet
Elevation Gain: 550 feet
Round Trip to Peak: 13 miles
Hiking Time: 6–7 hours
High Point: 6870 feet
Elevation Gain: 1300 feet
Maps: USGS Pole Mountain, Mallard Peak
Best Hiking Time: July to October
Contact: Idaho Panhandle National Forests (St. Joe), Avery Ranger District, (208) 245-4517

Driving Directions: From St. Maries, Idaho, follow the St. Joe River Road (Forest Road 50) east towards Avery. Beyond Avery, and after 75 long but scenic miles, come to a junction with FR 218. Bear right. (This junction can also be accessed from St. Regis, Montana, by following the Little Joe Road, FR 282, which becomes paved FR 50 once in Idaho, for 29 miles.) Proceed on FR 218 and follow it for 7 miles to the Beaver Creek Campground. Turn right just after the campground and cross the St. Joe River. Drive 8 slow miles up FR 303 (Beaver Creek Road). Four-wheel drive is not necessary but high clearance is. FR 303 ends on a high saddle at a junction with FR 201. Turn left (south) and drive this equally slow road for 7 miles to Table Camp, where this hike begins. The 15-mile drive to Table Camp from Beaver Creek Campground on the St. Joe River will take an hour.

This hike is recommended for dogs (and their humans) who don't mind shaking, rattling, and rolling before they even get to the trailhead. You'll be rewarded with some incredibly wild country. This hike acts as a sampler

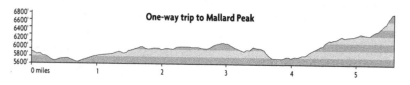

One-way trip to Mallard Peak

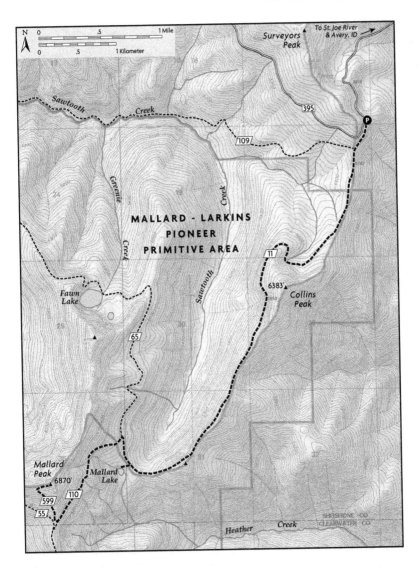

to the 32,000-acre Mallard-Larkins Pioneer Primitive Area, a federal wilderness candidate awaiting the magic wand (or congressional wand). Straddling the boundary between the Clearwater and St. Joe national forests, the Mallard-Larkins Pioneer Primitive Area consists of some of the most rugged country north of the Clearwater River. Craggy peaks rise above 7000 feet, with a score of alpine lakes scattered between them. Mountain goats climb along the cliffs.

Baby moose

The primitive access road limits the number of visitors, making this a good place to escape the crowds. Consider camping at the primitive but nicely situated Table Camp, allowing you more time to explore adjacent trails, ridges, and lakes.

Mallard Lake is perhaps the easiest lake to get to in the Mallard-Larkins Pioneer country. Sure, it's a 10.5-mile round trip, but you only climb 550 feet. Much of the route crosses a level ridge. If you have a little energy left after getting to the lake, consider trekking to Mallard Peak. The extra 3 miles will cost you a little more effort, but it's still a fairly easy ascent.

From Table Camp (water available in nearby creeks) follow Trail 11 south. After 0.25 mile you'll come to FR 201. Turn left and briefly walk this road until you see a sign pointing out the trail to your left. Through a forest of mountain hemlock, begin descending to a saddle on the ridge. Pass the junction with Sawtooth Creek Trail 49 (which leads west into the Sawtooth Creek valley) and commence hiking on a wonderful ridgeline through old-growth forest.

In 1.25 miles you'll come a creek crossing, saturated with shooting stars in early summer. On the west side of the ridge, openings in the forest grant views out to Snow and Sawtooth Peaks. Mallard Peak soon comes into view.

In 3 miles you'll reach an open area with fine views of Mallard Peak. The lake sits in a high basin to the east. Sawtooth Creek roars far below in the valley. In 4 miles you'll drop to a forested basin that often harbors snow well into July. After 5 miles a spur trail leads left to Larkins Lake. Look for a weathered sign pointing the way.

Larkins Lake sits in a small bowl just below Larkins Peak. It's a pretty spot with a grassy shoreline that invites loitering (if the mosquitoes haven't yet arrived). Your dog will enjoy snooping around and will probably be as fascinated as you are by the hundreds of frogs that call this lake home. It's a hopping place!

If you desire to carry on, head back to the main trail and continue for a short way to a junction with Trail 110. Turn left and ascend open ledges to the 6870-foot summit. The historic fire tower is worth exploring. Enjoy sweeping views of this wild country while deciding which lake to explore next.

BITTERROOT DIVIDE

58. Settlers Grove Cedars-West Fork Eagle Creek

Location: Coeur d'Alene River
Round Trip: 5 miles
Hiking Time: 3 hours
High Point: 4000 feet
Elevation Gain: 700 feet
Map: USGS Murray
Best Hiking Time: May through October
Contact: Idaho Panhandle National Forests (Coeur d'Alene), Coeur d'Alene River Ranger District, (208) 664-2318

Driving Directions: From Coeur d'Alene, Idaho, head east on Interstate 90 to the Kingston exit 43. Follow Forest Road 9 (Coeur d'Alene River Road) east for 23 miles to the little settlement of Prichard. After crossing Prichard Creek, come to a junction. Turn right, continuing on FR 9 towards Thompson Pass (the road straight, FR 208, leads to the Coeur d'Alene River Trail, Hike 53). In 2.75 miles you'll come to what remains of the town of Eagle. Turn left (north) onto County Road 152, also known as Eagle Creek Road. Following signs for Settlers Grove, in 1.4

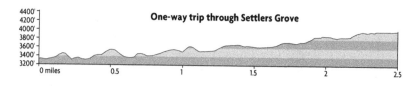

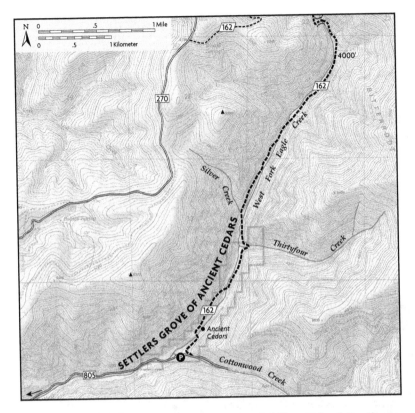

miles make a left-hand turn onto FR 805 and follow it for 5.5 miles to its end. The trail begins here from a large parking area.

Judging by the large parking lot and the big-beamed arch that denotes the beginning of this trail, you'd guess that this is a popular hike. It is, but for only the first 0.5 mile. The overwhelming majority of hikers who come to the Settlers Grove of Ancient Cedars ramble only to the first few giants. Beyond the well-constructed portion of trail that accommodates these tree gazers is a lightly used trail that delivers even more groves of giant cedars and a plethora of American dippers. If these flitting, diving, water-loving birds aren't enough to hold the attention of you and your canine, then perhaps the ruins of an old mining operation will.

Trail 162 begins as a well-developed nature path complete with a gravel surface and railed bridges spanning the West Fork of Eagle Creek. Although it's not required, your buddy should be leashed for this section due to the number of visitors. Once beyond the sign that states "End of

Mittens and her human in Settlers Grove area, West Fork Eagle Creek

cedar grove trail," it's okay for your pal to hike unrestrained.

Settlers Grove is a beautiful place. Ancient western red cedars with stocky girths and burled, fluted, and hollowed trunks grace the narrow valley, reducing you and your dog to Lilliputian status. You'll walk with your head cocked towards the canopy high above. More than likely, though, your dog won't be fazed by all this biomass. She'll be more interested in sniffing out the native critters. Perhaps she'll spot a toad. One of the biggest I have ever seen lives in this grove.

In 0.5 mile the route leaves the crowds behind on a true backcountry trail. Begin journeying up the West Fork of Eagle Creek. The trail alternates between hugging its banks and rising slightly above it, but always within eyesight and earshot of the water.

Big cedars continue to line the way, with giant hemlocks interspersed. In 1.5 miles, before a bridge over the creek, you'll find a good campsite—an excellent observation post for dipper watching. Across the creek some small scree slopes offer views of the surrounding hoodoos.

In 2.5 miles the trail crosses a bridge back to the west side of the creek. Beyond this the trail climbs (sometimes steeply and across scree) from the creek to attain the Bitterroot Divide. It's possible via the Trout Creek Trail to hike down the other side of the divide into Montana.

But for most day hikers and their dogs this is a good turnaround. Before you do so, be sure to walk a few hundred feet off the trail up the creek bank, where you'll find the ruins of an old cabin and mining operation. You'll also find a nice spot to sit by the creek. Relish the fact that despite past human endeavors, the West Fork of Eagle Creek is still a wild place.

59. Revett Lake

Location: Bitterroot Mountains
Round Trip: 4 miles
Hiking Time: 2 hours
High Point: 5700 feet
Elevation Gain: 500 feet
Maps: USGS Burke, Thompson Pass
Best Hiking Time: July through October
Contact: Idaho Panhandle National Forests (Coeur d'Alene), Coeur d'Alene River Ranger District, (208) 664-2318

Driving Directions: From Coeur d'Alene, Idaho, head east on Interstate 90 to the Kingston exit 43. Follow Forest Road 9 (Coeur d'Alene River Road) east for 38 miles all the way to Thompson Pass. Be sure to note the intersection in Prichard (at 23 miles), where FR 9 makes a sharp right

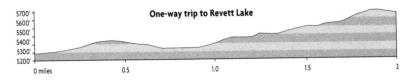

to Murray. At Thompson Pass, turn right into the large parking area/ scenic pull-out. Proceed to FR 266 at the south end of the pull-out and follow it 1.2 miles to the trailhead. Thompson Pass can also be reached from the east. From Thompson Falls, Montana, follow FR 7 (Prospect Creek Road) west for 22 miles.

Yet another aquatic jewel located high along the Bitterroot Divide that separates Idaho from Montana, pretty little Revett Lake is nestled in a bowl below 6814-foot Granite Peak. The lake's surroundings are subalpine; ridges of talus and meadows rise above the tranquil body of water, forests of fir and spruce ring the rocky shoreline. This is as beautiful a spot as any in the Bitterroots. But you don't have to earn it—the hike to Revett is one of the easiest in these parts.

Naturally this hike gets some traffic. That shouldn't discourage you from bringing along your furry friend, especially if he's new to hiking, for Revett gets a fair amount of first-time hikers, tenderfoot backpackers, and fledgling trail pups. It's the perfect hike for weaning Rover from the backyard. Two miles of gentle trail and only 500 feet of elevation gain will hardly make him pant. Old-growth forest and the tumbling waters of Cascade Gulch will further keep his tongue from hanging out too far.

Plenty of friendly hikers and their dogs will welcome your buddy to this lake. But remember that it is always good to have him leashed. There

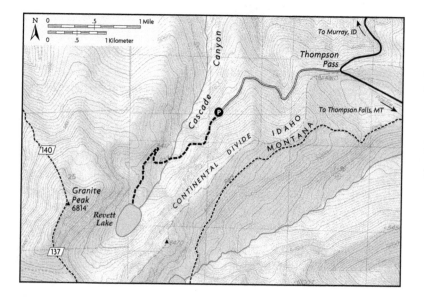

Jax and Jon along Revett Lake shore (Photo by Craig Romano)

are often a good number of children on this hike and there's always the chance of encountering a skittish dog.

The hike starts in a cool forest of hemlock and fir. Alternating between forest and open talus, the trail stays to the west of the divide, then drops gently to cross Revett's outlet stream. From there it's one big switchback and final delivery to the lake basin. Scope out a good campsite or a lunch rock—there are plenty near the outlet.

A two-year-old black Lab, Jax, from Kellogg, Idaho, found Revett to his liking for his very first hike. The cool waters were great for a swim, the shoreline rocks were great for a view, and the trail was a great leg stretcher. Fellow hikers and dogs welcomed him to the lake.

Perhaps he'll be ready next for the hike to nearby Blossom Lakes. It starts right from Thompson Pass and is only a mile longer.

60. Lone Lake

Location: Bitterroot Mountains
Round Trip: 4.5 miles
Hiking Time: 3 hours
High Point: 5550 feet
Elevation Gain: 1550 feet
Map: USGS Mullan
Best Hiking Time: May through October
Contact: Idaho Panhandle National Forests (Coeur d'Alene), Coeur d'Alene River Ranger District, (208) 664-2318

Driving Directions: From Kellogg, Idaho, take Interstate 90 east to exit 69 for East Mullan. Turn left (north), cross the freeway, then turn right on old highway 10 (signed for Shoshone Park). In 1 mile bear right onto Willow Creek Road, crossing back over the freeway and emerging at a crazy six-way intersection in 1.75 miles. Park here along an abandoned railroad bed, now part of the Forest Service road system. The hike begins up the road leading south on the right (west) side of Willow Creek. Do not drive up this road—it's gated within 500 feet.

A whole slew of alpine lakes dot the high country above Lookout Pass on the Bitterroot Divide that separates Idaho from Montana. The St. Regis Lakes are probably the most popular. Stevens Lake is the largest. Lone Lake is perhaps, well, the loneliest, which makes it an ideal destination for you and your hiking hound.

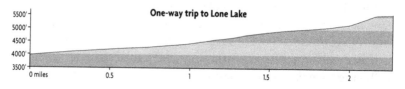

One-way trip to Lone Lake

Before setting off for this aquatic gem perched high in an open cirque below 6838-foot Stevens Peak, a bit of less-than-ideal terrain must be negotiated. As of 2004 a large logging operation has been in progress on the lower reaches of this hike, in essence obliterating the lower one-third of the trail. The trail is, however, still open; you just need to walk the new skid road to access it. You'll want to check when logging is occurring (or completed).

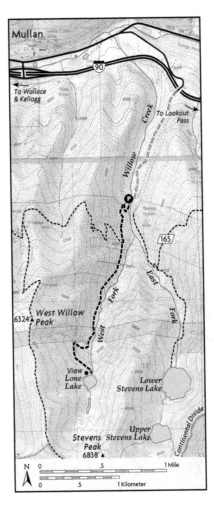

The hike begins on what will be a road for some time. Pass the gate and follow this road as it angles to the north and then continues on a mostly southern route, parallel to Willow Creek. A few signs on remaining trees point the way. At the end of the newly cut area (about 1 mile from the trailhead), follow the skid road that climbs away from the creek at about a 45-degree angle. Find the trail, an old road leading steeply up the forested valley. Soon the route resembles a bona fide trail and after 0.5 mile of steep going delivers you into a beautiful open area kept tree-free by avalanches.

The West Fork of Willow Creek, Lone Lake's outlet source, cascades off a ledge, providing a pretty backdrop to this lush and green environment. Climb a big, sweeping switchback to reach the lake above the cascade. The views north are good, to East Mullan in the Silver Valley and the lofty peaks that hem it in. Look for mining shafts on the open slopes of the ridge to the east.

In 2.25 miles you'll reach Lone Lake. An inviting shoreline, a hidden little lake above it, lingering snowfields, and wide-open slopes encircling

G.G. in Lone Lake

it invite further exploration. There's a small campsite by the outlet and a big lunch rock nearby.

61. Crystal Lake

Location: Bitterroot Mountains
Round Trip: 3.5 miles
Hiking Time: 3 hours
High Point: 5500 feet
Elevation Gain: 1400 feet
Map: USGS Haugan SW
Best Hiking Time: June through October
Contact: Lolo National Forest, Superior Ranger District, (406) 822-4233

Driving Directions: From Interstate 90 take exit 18 for DeBorgia, Montana. Upon exiting immediately turn right (if coming from the east,

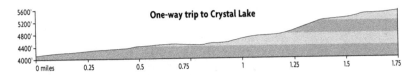

turn left) onto a dirt road. Immediately turn right again and proceed west on this dirt road, paralleling I-90. In 0.5 mile the road crosses the St. Regis River, becoming Deer Creek Road (Forest Road 236). Head south for 5.75 miles, coming to a gate and the trailhead for Crystal Lake Trail 269.

The hike to Crystal Lake is short but steep—in elevation and in history. It's not a terribly difficult hike, just a bit of a grunt for short-winded dogs and their owners. At least the trail, which utilizes an old mining road for most of the way, is shaded, and there's no shortage of water. Crystal's deep waters invite a swim, and its rocky shoreline is a great place to soak

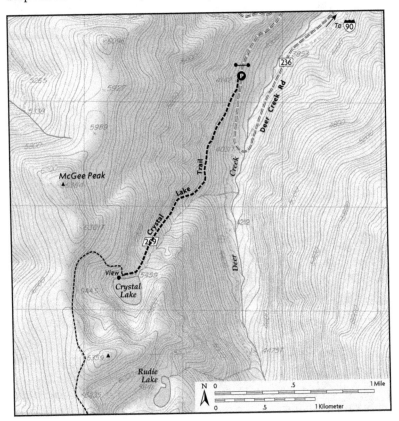

Mike Raether and Nugget on trail to Crystal Lake

up the sun. A former mining town site will interest two-legged visitors, while hounds will enjoy sniffing out the faunal past.

The hike starts on an old road nicely converted to trail. Ignore the trailhead sign that states "Crystal Lake 4.5 miles." It may feel that long, but it's closer to 1.5 miles. The trail makes it way through a cool forest of cedar, spruce, and the occasional white pine. Plenty of babbling brooks are crossed, all feeding Deer Creek below.

In 0.5 mile the trail steepens. There are a few rocky spots, victims of erosion. In 1.25 miles the grade eases and the trail enters the site of the former Deer Creek Mining Company Town. You'll see the remains of several cabins and tailings from the mines. The gold ran out in 1913 and the town dissolved. The forest has been reclaiming the area ever since.

Half a mile beyond the town site, you'll reach Crystal Lake. Here, too, you will see relics from the past. The lake's waters were once used to harness power—notice the three flumes leading from its outlet, and the pilings nearby. A century ago this tranquil body of water was bustling with activity. Today it greets hikers and anglers looking for peace and quiet. Good campsites abound if you're inclined to stay the night. The trail itself continues higher into the Bitterroots.

62. Hazel and Hub Lakes

Location: Bitterroot Mountains
Round Trip: 6 miles
Hiking Time: 4 hours
High Point: 5720 feet
Elevation Gain: 1700 feet
Map: USGS DeBorgia S
Best Hiking Time: late June through mid-October
Contact: Lolo National Forest, Superior Ranger District, (406) 822-4233

Driving Directions: From St. Regis, Montana, travel west on Interstate 90 to exit 25, signed "Drexel." Get back on I-90 and head east to exit 26, signed "Ward Creek." (You can only use this exit eastbound.) If coming from the west, use exit 26. (After your hike, to go back west you'll

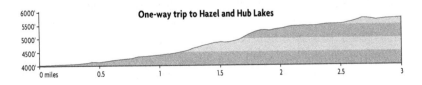

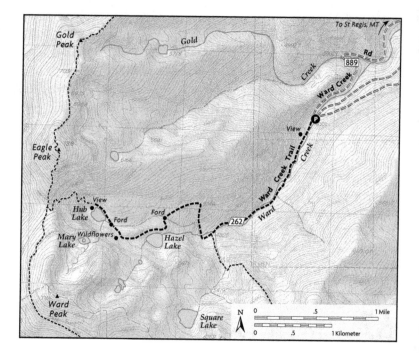

have to travel eastbound on I-90 to exit 28 and then reverse direction.) From exit 26 travel south on Ward Creek Road (Forest Road 889) for 6.25 miles to where the road makes a sharp turn left, crossing Ward Creek. The trail begins here. There is parking for a few vehicles on either side of Ward Creek.

This is a great hike to two lovely backcountry lakes tucked along the Bitterroot Divide, which separates Idaho from Montana. En route you and your pooch will be treated to a cool forest of old growth cedars, a scenic overlook of crashing Dipper Falls, and a couple of paw-splashing creek crossings. Hazel is the larger and closer lake, but Hub is more scenic and offers better fishing, swimming, and camping.

Follow Ward Creek Trail 262 through a lush cedar forest, marveling at some of the old giants that escaped the Great Fire of 1910, which engulfed three million surrounding acres. After some easy going the trail begins to climb. Pause for a few minutes to gaze out at Dipper Falls. Perhaps you'll even see a dipper or two at the base of the 60-foot cataract.

In 1.25 miles you'll come to a junction. Turn right here onto the Hazel-Hub Lake Trail 280. The grade eases as you make a long switchback up to the lake basins. At about 2.25 miles you'll have to cross the tributary coming down from Hub Lake. In early summer plan on getting your paws wet.

Soon you'll come to another trail junction. The left path drops steeply to tranquil Hazel Lake. There is a good campsite, but the shoreline is brushy and views are limited.

Continue to Hub Lake. It's about 0.5 mile further via a climb through meadows, a drop through forest, and another paw-soaking creek crossing. Once you emerge to the high basin that houses Hub Lake, you'll realize the slight discomfort was worth it.

Hub sits in a semi-open bowl. Cliffs and high meadows from towering Ward and Eagle Peaks hem it in. There are good campsites near the outlet and at the far end of the lake. A classic lunch rock can be found by following the trail a little way along the shore. Your dog will remind you that the rock makes for a good launching pad into the lake.

The trail continues to Up Up Ridge where both the summits of Eagle and Ward can be accessed. The climb out of the basin is extremely steep and not recommended for most happy-go-lucky hounds. Opt instead to

Hub Lake with view to Ward Peak

while away the time by soaking up the sun and scenery from pretty little Hub, the absolute center to this gorgeous basin.

63. Diamond and Cliff Lakes

Location: Bitterroot Mountains
Round Trip: 3 miles
Hiking Time: 2 hours
High Point: 5900 feet
Elevation Gain: 500 feet
Map: USGS Illinois Peak NW
Best Hiking Time: June to October
Contact: Lolo National Forest, Superior Ranger District, (406) 822-4233

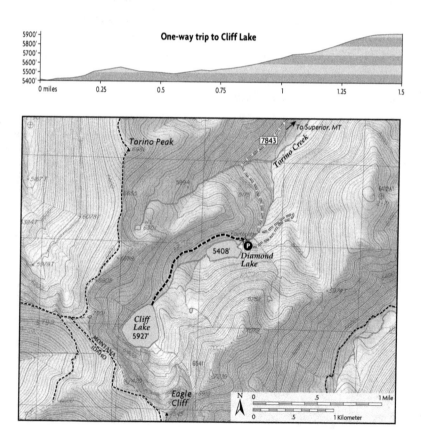

Cliff Lake nestled in the Bitterroot Mountain Divide

Driving Directions: From Superior, Montana, travel west on Interstate 90 to exit 43. Head south on the Frontage Road (County Road 69) for 1 mile. Make a sharp right turn onto Dry Creek Road (signed "Forest Service Road 342—Diamond Lake 13 miles"). After 0.5 mile the surface changes to gravel. Continue for 9 miles until you come to the junction with Forest Road 7843. Turn left onto this narrow gravel road and follow it 4 miles to its end at Diamond Lake. The trail begins behind the gate.

The Bitterroot Divide between Idaho and Montana contains scores of beautiful backcountry lakes. Two of the most accessible are Diamond and Cliff. No surprise, then, that these two lakes see a fair amount of visitors. But this is western Montana, not western Washington, so "crowded" is still an unknown word here. On a Fourth of July hike to these gems, I shared the trail and the shoreline with only six other parties and four other dogs!

This is a social trail, a place where neophyte backpackers test their gear (and backs), and a great place to bring Rover on his first hike. Since other dogs are on the trail it's a good idea to have yours on a leash.

The trail begins behind the gate at the bridge over Torino Creek. There are campsites here for those who want to car camp. Continue past the camping area on Cliff Lake Trail 100. Following an old road, the trail gradually climbs above Diamond Lake. Soon the route becomes a bona fide trail and crosses a sprawling avalanche zone. There are good views of Diamond down below, as well as brilliant floral shows, including fields of larkspur and a boggy section filled with elephant's head.

Beyond the avalanche chutes the trail enters a cool forest and continues alongside tumbling Torino Creek. After 1.25 miles and 500 feet of climbing you'll emerge at appropriately named Cliff Lake. The rock flanks of Eagle Cliff form an imposing wall along the lake's south side.

There's camping beside the outlet, but these sites tend to be abused. For secluded sites, nice lunch rocks, and great scenery, follow the well-beaten path along the lake's eastern shore for about 0.25 mile. Here, in a field littered with big boulders and blotched with patches of snow, you and your buddy can play and explore. You can swim, too, but the snowmelt draining into Cliff Lake may deter you. Your dog may have to paddle alone.

64. Heart and Pearl Lakes

Location: Bitterroot Mountains
Round Trip: 8 miles
Hiking Time: 5 hours
High Point: 6262 feet
Elevation Gain: 1600 feet
Maps: USGS Straight Peak NW, Hoodoo Pass
Best Hiking Time: late June through mid-October
Contact: Lolo National Forest, Superior Ranger District, (406) 822-4233

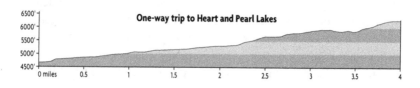

One-way trip to Heart and Pearl Lakes

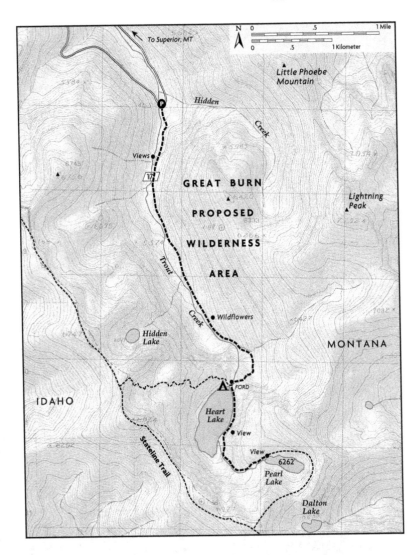

Driving Directions: From Superior, Montana, (exit 47 on Interstate 90) head east on Diamond Road (County Road 257), a paved road which becomes gravel after 6 miles. Pass Trout Creek Campground and after 20 miles find the trailhead for Heart Lake on your left. Parking is on the opposite side of the road.

The hike to Heart Lake, one of the largest bodies of water in the Bitterroot Mountains, is satisfying, but it only scratches the surface of

Pearl Lake nestled in the Bitterroot Mountain Divide

the adventure to be had in this area. Most hikers rarely wander off the main artery, though there are half a dozen other amazing lakes and miles of high, uncrowded ridges.

Trail 171 enters a cool forest of subalpine fir and Engelmann spruce. Look closer and you'll notice that these tall trees stand in stark contrast to much of the surrounding landscape, which sports silver snags, ground-hugging shrubs, and golden grasses. This entire area was engulfed in a massive wildfire a century ago, and nature is slowly regenerating. All this newly created open country has provided good forage for big beasties. All of this area has remained roadless and is being considered for inclusion in a 250,000-acre federally protected Great Burn Wilderness Area.

This creekside trail works its way up the valley. Some brushy avalanche areas must be traversed (watch for nettles), but most of the route is under forest canopy. A lot of small critters such as hares, squirrels, and snakes (but not the poisonous ones) will keep your dog alert.

At 2 miles the route crosses a creek on a log, and 0.25 mile further another creek must be forded. Soon after you'll come to a junction. Take the trail left to Pearl Lake. The trail right is a continuation of the Heart Lake Trail but it doesn't go to the lake; instead it climbs 1.5 miles to the Stateline Trail high on the Bitterroot Divide.

In a short 0.25 mile you'll emerge at the logjammed outlet of Heart Lake. Enjoy the cool breezes coming off the sparkling waters and the view of the cirque walls that tower above the lake. Sit, splash, or munch—then continue to Pearl. Follow the trail along the eastern shore of the lake for 0.5 mile. There are a few rocky spots that may require assisting your canine friend.

At the south end of Heart Lake, the trail turns east and begins a series of short switchbacks up a steep grassy slope. There are good views out over Heart. A little over a mile from Heart's outlet you'll enter the high grassy bowl that houses Pearl Lake. It's much more shallow than Heart, therefore much warmer. There are some campsites by the outlet, but there's no protection in stormy weather.

If you and your dog have plenty of energy, continue on the trail to a high saddle above. From there you can drop down to isolated Dalton Lake or continue climbing, eventually meeting the Stateline Trail. It's possible to travel north to meet up with the Heart Lake Trail and make a 12-mile loop. But beware, there are lots of ups and downs, no water once the snow has melted, and full exposure to the sun and weather.

CABINET MOUNTAINS

65. Calder Mountain–Pend Oreille Divide

Location: Cabinet Mountains
Round Trip: 8.5 miles
Hiking Time: 6 hours
High Point: 5701 feet
Elevation Gain: 1900 feet
Map: USGS Mount Pend Oreille NW
Best Hiking Time: June through October
Contact: Idaho Panhandle National Forests (Kaniksu), Sandpoint
Ranger District, (208) 263-5111

Driving Directions: From Sandpoint, Idaho, drive east on State Route 200 for 6 miles to Colburn-Culver Road (at milepost 36). Turn left. After 6 miles cross Grouse Creek and turn right onto County Road 794. Proceed 0.75 mile, then turn right onto Grouse Creek Road. Follow this gravel road 4.25 miles to a junction. Bear right onto Forest Road 280 and follow it 8 miles to the road's end, where you'll find a large parking area and the trailhead.

The 13-mile Pend Oreille Divide Trail offers some of the finest ridgeline walking within the entire Cabinet Range. Undulating between 5000 and

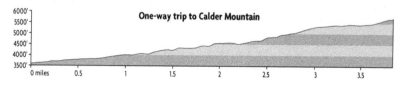

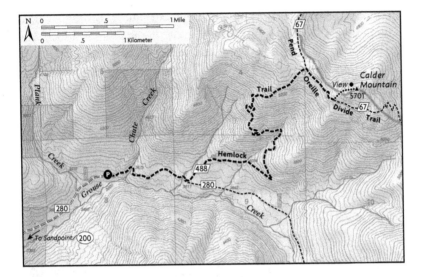

6700 feet, this skyline trail traverses sprawling alpine meadows, skirts lonely windblown summits, and provides almost nonstop views of the Selkirk Crest, massive Lake Pend Oreille, and the craggy Montana Cabinets. Unfortunately, the divide is as dry as a dog bone (sans saliva), making it a most difficult trek for both two- and four-legged adventurers.

However, a taste of the divide can be had in relative ease via the 3.75-mile Hemlock Trail. The trail is well-maintained, there's water along the way, huckleberries galore in season, and all those aforementioned views.

Hemlock Trail 488 starts off as an old road. The first mile is pleasant, crossing several creeks that flow well into the summer. After 1.5 miles of easy going, you'll pass your last reliable water source and begin ascending a series of short switchbacks. It's a good little grunt up a southern slope. If it's late in the morning, the two of you will be panting. At 2.5 miles you'll enter a mature forest, and in 3 miles the grade eases and the trail breaks into a lovely meadow.

In 3.75 miles you'll come to a signed junction with the Pend Oreille Divide Trail (5400 ft.). For those promised views, travel south on the Divide Trail for about 10 minutes until you break into a small south-facing meadow. Leave the trail and head northeast through the meadows. In 10 minutes and 300 more feet of climbing you'll reach the 5701-foot summit of Calder Mountain.

Break out the water bottles, the gorp, and the kibble. Soak up a spectacular 360-degree panoramic view. Montana's Snowshoe and A peaks dominate the west. Mount Clifty and the Katka Ridge form an emerald wall to the north. Lake Pend Oreille sparkles in the southwest while the Pend Oreille Ridge, with its wave of summits, marches into the southeastern horizon. When you tire of the views, make the easy return, but don't forget to allot some time for huckleberry harvesting. Your hound can always nap in the meadows.

Sherlock among huckleberries, Pend Oreille Divide

66. Moose Lake and Mountain

Location: Cabinet Mountains
Round Trip: 7 miles
Hiking Time: 4 hours
High Point: 6543 feet
Elevation Gain: 1640 feet
Map: USGS Mount Pend Oreille
Best Hiking Time: mid-June to mid-October
Contact: Idaho Panhandle National Forests (Kaniksu), Sandpoint
Ranger District, (208) 263-5111

Driving Directions: From Sandpoint, Idaho, drive east on State Route
200 for 12 miles. Just beyond milepost 42, turn left (north) on Forest
Road 275 (Trestle Creek Road). Drive 16 bumpy and slow miles to FR
419 (Lightning Creek). Turn left and follow FR 419. In 1 mile come to a
bridge over Lightning Creek, and 0.25 mile beyond the bridge make a
sharp right onto FR 1022 (Moose Creek). Follow this even bumpier road
2.25 miles to its end at the Moose Lake Trailhead.

Hike to a quiet alpine lake nestled in the western range of the Cabinet
Mountains. When you and your dog tire of lying on the sunny shoreline
or splashing in the warm shallows, head to an even quieter summit, complete with views that overlook the lake and everything else within a 50-
mile radius. Best of all, this hike is easy, even for a tired old hound. And,
yes, there are moose here, so make sure your faithful friend stays close.

Trail 237 immediately heads into open woods. Breaks in the forest canopy
provide limited views of the surrounding ridges. Moose Creek tumbles alongside the wide and gentle trail. In 0.5 mile stay left at a signed junction. The
trail to the right leads 2.5 miles to Blacktail Lake, also a worthy destination.
In 10 minutes you'll come to a second junction. Take the trail to the right;
the one on the left leads 2.5 miles to Lake Estelle, yet another option.

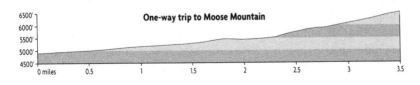

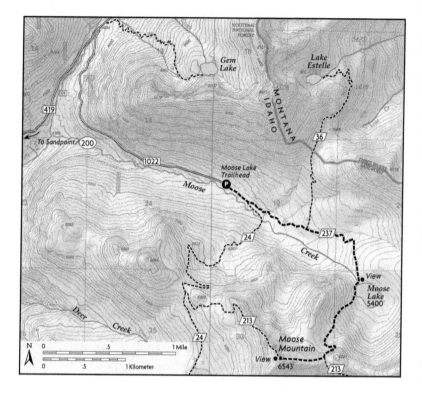

After 20 minutes you and your furry friend will enter the semi-open basin housing Moose Lake (5400 ft.), ringed by a grassy marshy shore. Your dog won't mind taking a dip, although you may hesitate. In early summer hordes of mosquitoes may force a quick visit, but as the autumn equinox approaches, Moose Lake becomes quite hospitable. Don't get too comfortable, though, for the surrounding ridge calls out to be explored.

If the two of you are inclined to go further, head to Moose Mountain, the site of an old lookout. Near the lake's outlet, find the abandoned trail to the mountain. Cross the outlet on a sturdy log, then pick up the trail near the lake's southern shore. The route is a little overgrown, but easy to follow. Keep an eye out for moose in the surrounding bogs.

The trail leaves the lake and begins a short, steep climb. Cross another boggy area, the last reliable water, and work your way across a small scree slope. About 40 minutes from the lake you'll reach a saddle on the ridge (6300 ft.). Do not continue down the other side of it; instead, look for an old sign hanging in a tree. Turn right and head up the spine of the ridge leading to the summit of Moose Mountain. Cairns lead the way and it's fairly obvious. In about 15 minutes from the ridge gap you'll reach the 6543-foot summit.

Time now to soak up the views of the lake; it twinkles directly below you. Peer out at the wild country all around you—the largest unprotected tract of wilderness left in the Cabinets. The ragged bone-dry Pend Oreille Divide stretches out to the north. The Selkirk Crest sprawls across the western horizon. To the south, 7009-foot Scotchman Peak towers over its neighbors. The snow-capped and rugged Montana Cabinets dominate the view to the east.

It's possible to continue on the abandoned Moose Mountain Trail down the western side and to the Blacktail Trail for a 7-mile loop. However, beware—maps still show the trail, but it has all but vanished in several sections. Route-finding skills are a must.

Moose foraging through wet leaves

67. Little Spar Lake

Location: Cabinet Mountains
Round Trip: 8 miles
Hiking Time: 6 hours
High Point: 5239 feet
Elevation Gain: 1800 feet
Maps: Spar Lake, USGS Mount Pend Oreille
Best Hiking Time: July through October
Contact: Kootenai National Forest, Three Rivers Ranger District, (406) 295-4693

Driving Directions: From Troy, Montana, follow US Highway 2 east to Lake Creek Road at milepost 16 just before a highway rest area. Turn right (south) and follow Lake Creek Road, which becomes Forest Road 384, for 17 miles to Spar Lake Campground (follow signs). Proceed 2 rough miles beyond the campground, cross Spar Creek and arrive at the trailhead. There is parking for about a dozen vehicles.

Little Spar Lake sits in a rugged basin within the shadows of 7009-foot Scotchman Peak. The trail to it travels through groves of giant cedars, skirts below cliffs, and blazes across wildlife-rich meadows. This is some of the finest country in the Cabinet Mountains and is worthy of federal wilderness designation. Perhaps after you and your dog trek to this alpine gem you'll bark to your legislators about fully protecting it.

Little Spar makes for a good backpacking destination if you come during the week. Although certainly not a busy place compared to some of the Idaho Selkirk Lakes, there can be more than a few pups doing the dog paddle here on a warm Saturday in July. On a quiet weeknight, the lake can be the sole property of you and your best friend. There are good camping spots by the outlet, fine swimming, and superb high-country roaming. Remember to be bear-aware.

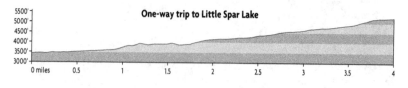

One-way trip to Little Spar Lake

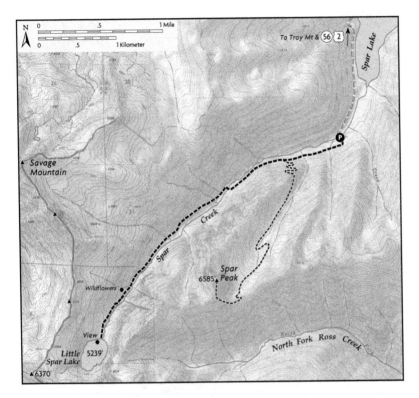

Trail 143 starts off as old road, rocky and rutted but easy enough to negotiate with two or four feet. Massive cedars line the former logging road. In less than a 0.5 mile the trail to Spar Mountain takes off left. This is a shorter but much more difficult trail, and the payoff is in the panoramic views.

Just beyond the Spar Mountain Trail junction, turn left on the real trail (signed), leaving the old road once and for all. A cool and refreshing hemlock forest greets you, and a hot and brushy alder thicket extends the welcome. In 1.5 miles there is a crossing of Spar Creek, which may be difficult in early summer. During the dog days of summer, yours will seek the creek's refreshing qualities.

For the next 2.5 miles the trail stays within earshot of Spar Creek descending from its source, lovely Spar Lake. Big trees gradually give way to meadows created by massive avalanches. An avalanche in the winter of 2003 cut a swath across the trail. It's not uncommon to encounter snow in this valley well into summer. Your dog will likely plop down in it like

Hikers relax on the shore of Little Spar Lake.

a mountain goat. And speaking of goats, while your pooch takes a breather, scan the cliffs above.

In about 3.5 miles you'll pass by some picturesque cascades. The meadows end and it's just one final push to the lake, which you reach at 4 miles. Enter the cirque, scope out a warm rock, and kick back. Your dog, however, may already be in the lake. Consider joining him, for by late summer, furless hikers can enjoy Spar's waters as well.

68. Little Ibex Lake

Location: Cabinet Mountains
Round Trip: 12 miles
Hiking Time: 8 hours
High Point: 5170 feet
Elevation Gain: 2700 feet
Maps: Cabinet Mountains Wilderness USFS, Ibex Peak USGS
Best Hiking Time: July to October
Contact: Kootenai National Forest, Cabinet Ranger District,
(406) 827-3534

Driving Directions: From Sandpoint, Idaho, follow State Route 200 east to junction with Montana SR 56 (10 miles east of the Idaho-Montana border). Travel north on SR 56 for 16 miles. Turn right (east) onto Forest Road 410 (South Fork Bull River Road) and follow signs for Middle Fork Bull River Trail 978. Two miles from SR 56 turn left onto FR 2722. In 0.5 mile bear right. In another 0.25 mile turn right on a short spur road (sign indicating trail), and follow it 0.1 mile to the trailhead.

The Cabinet Mountain Wilderness is a striking land of snow-capped, cloud-piercing peaks, deep valleys of towering primeval trees, and sparkling alpine lakes. Word is spreading quickly about the Cabinets. Hence, many a high-country Cabinet Mountain lake is seeing a surge in visitors. Not true for Little Ibex Lake, though. For although Little Ibex ranks among the most scenic places in the entire wilderness, it remains little known and rarely visited.

Why? For one thing Little Ibex is tucked away on the western side of the range, far from the main trails and access. Secondly, the trek to the lake requires 6 miles and 2700 feet of climbing, and half of the ascent is made in the last 2 miles. Thirdly, a difficult river ford is required. Furthermore, the trail to the lake sees little maintenance and is littered with

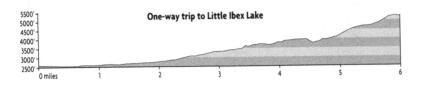

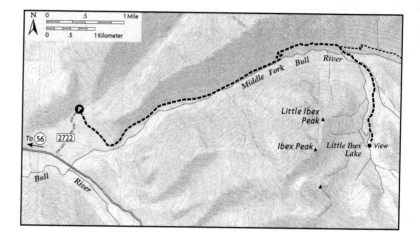

windfall. However, it's still fairly easy to follow. Most of the downed trees are small and low to the ground, and it's easy enough for you and your dog (unless he's a dachshund) to negotiate.

Begin your sojourn on Trail 978 along the pristine Middle Fork of the Bull River. You'll first travel across lush river bottomlands, through dark cedar forests, and across a wayward channel or two. Watch for moose and deer. The Cabinets are also home to a handful of grizzlies, but much of the habitat along this hike is not prime bear country. Still, it's best to make your presence known. Keep your companion nearby, and bark to each other.

In about 2 miles you'll pass a giant glacial erratic. The trail now hugs the river. There are lots of soothing spots for camping, splashing, and resting. Enter the wilderness and continue along a gorgeous section of the river, overflowing with cascades. At 3 miles there's a small climb across a scree slope, followed by more cool forest glades.

In 4 miles you'll come to a cairn in the trail, the turnoff for Little Ibex Lake (3800 ft.). This junction is not signed and the path to the right isn't obvious at first. Drop down to the river and look for a safe place to ford. If the river is too high or dangerous, skip the lake and continue up the Middle Fork Trail for another 2 miles.

If you want to persevere to the lake, prepare for 2 miles of tough going. Once across the river the trail takes off left; Ibex Creek will be on your right. Immediately begin climbing on a rib between the Middle Fork Bull River and Ibex Creek. Despite the numerous downed trees, the route is easy to follow and well shaded. An easy stream crossing with pretty

Taking in the view at Little Ibex Lake (Photo by Craig Romano)

pools greets you at 4.75 miles. In another 0.5 mile you'll come to a muddy section of trail overgrown with ferns. Now the fun begins. The next 0.5 mile gains 800 steep feet of elevation.

Just when you can't bear any more, you'll crest the ridge and enter the lake basin (5170 ft.). For good campsites search high ground to the left. For spectacular views fight your way right through scrappy forest to the lake's outlet. Hop, skip, or jump across the outlet to an open boulder field on the lake's western shore.

The only thing that'll take your breath away faster than the view is a plunge in the lake. Plop your aching tailbones on a rock and soak up the surrounding landscape. Here in the heart of the Cabinet Mountains Wilderness, stark cliffs, hanging glaciers, and barren ridges enclose you. Lentz Peak (7298 ft.), adorned in rock and snow, reflects in Little Ibex's chilly waters. You'll not tire of the view. The hike, however, should tire the both of you quite thoroughly.

69. Saint Paul Lake

Location: Cabinet Mountains
Round Trip: 8 miles
Hiking Time: 5 hours
High Point: 4750 feet
Elevation Gain: 1600 feet
Maps: Cabinet Mountains Wilderness USFS, or Elephant Peak USGS
Best Hiking Time: July to October
Contact: Kootenai National Forest, Cabinet Ranger District,
(406) 827-3534

Driving Directions: From Sandpoint, Idaho, follow State Route 200 east to the junction with Montana SR 56 (10 miles east of Idaho-Montana border). Travel north on SR 56 for 8 miles. Turn right (east) onto Forest Road 407 (East Fork Bull River Road) and follow it for just shy of 6 miles to the trailhead.

This hike may very well be the top dog for canine hiking in the 94,000-acre Cabinet Mountains Wilderness. Why? A scenic, uncrowded lake, a well-groomed trail that hugs a bubbling creek for almost its entirety, and miles of cool and damp old-growth forest—what more could you ask for? Get Rover into the rig and head to the trail.

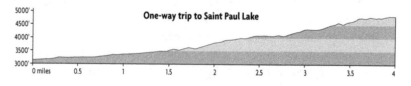

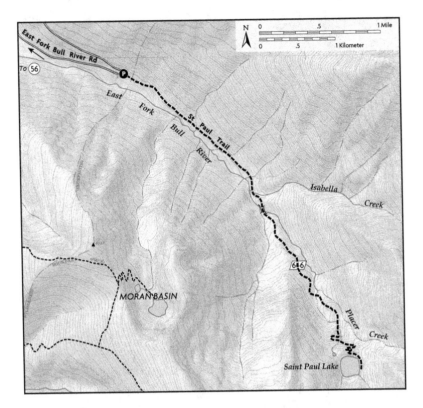

Saint Paul Trail 646 is a pure pleasure to hike for pups and old dogs alike. Even ol' Barkley, an arthritic blue heeler, made it, enjoying every creek crossing, swimming hole, and spring along the way. The trail immediately enters the wilderness and one of the finest old-growth cedar forests in the entire Inland Northwest. In 1.5 miles you'll come to an exceptional grove of giants, what I call "Saint Paul's Cathedral Forest." Here, too, is a lovely camping spot right on the East Fork of the Bull River.

Shortly beyond is Isabella Creek, which in high water can be tricky to cross. In about 2 miles you'll cross another creek, this time on a bridge. Your dog will probably bypass, however, heading for the cool pools. In 2.5 miles the grade increases and the trail begins to switchback. Huge cedars and hemlocks keep you shaded. Dense thickets of devil's club keep your pal from wandering off the trail.

The forest begins to thin out at about 3.0 miles, but the terrain remains lush. Your pup will be tempted to play in the mud holes. After one last steep climb you'll emerge on a bench above the lake. Make your

Autumn and Sasha on the shore of Saint Paul Lake (Photo by Craig Romano)

way down to quiet body of water via a somewhat brushy final 0.25 mile. Emerge into an open grassy basin with centerpiece Saint Paul Lake twinkling in the sunlight. Towering peaks encircle you. The sound of tumbling cascades fills this subalpine amphitheater.

Plan on spending some time here, perhaps even the night. The grassy shore is perfect for picnicking or napping. You'll both want to plunge into the warm waters of the lake. As I mentioned earlier, Saint Paul Lake is perhaps the best place in the Cabinet Mountain Wilderness for whiling away the dog days of summer.

70. Bramlet Lake

Location: Cabinet Mountains
Round Trip: 3 miles
Hiking Time: 2 hours
High Point: 5500 feet
Elevation Gain: 800 feet
Maps: USFS Cabinet Mountains Wilderness, or USGS Howard Lake
Best Hiking Time: late June to October
Contact: Kootenai National Forest, Libby Ranger District,
   (406) 293-8861 or (406) 827-3534

Driving Directions: From Libby, Montana, head east on US Highway
2 for 24 miles. Immediately before milepost 57 and the bridge across

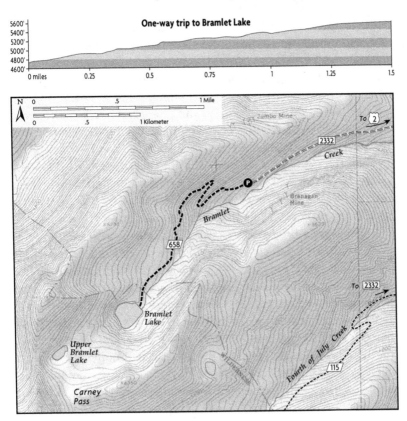

Elephant head growing on the shore of Bramlet Lake

Fisher River, turn right onto Forest Road 231 (West Fisher Creek Road). Follow this road for 5.5 miles and turn left on FR 2332. Proceed on this road 3.5 miles to the trailhead. The last 1.5 miles are rough and steep, warranting a high-clearance vehicle. If your car won't make it, park at the Fourth of July Trailhead and hike the road. This adds 3 miles and 900 feet of elevation to the hike.

Here's a short, sweet hike to a gem of a lake that doesn't get too busy. Little Bramlet Lake sits in a forested bowl just inside the Cabinet Mountains Wilderness. The trail to it, however, is outside of the wilderness. Once an old mining road, Trail 658 has reverted to trail. But the mining claims in the area are still active and this may complicate access to the area in the future. Be sure to check with the ranger station before venturing this way; there is a possibility that the trailhead may be moved.

From the trailhead it's a pretty straight shot to the lake. Beginning rather steeply, the trail gains 800 vertical feet in 1.5 miles. Bramlet Creek roars below you, but it's not easy to get to. You'll have to wait until you're near the lake before you get to admire the creek up close and personal.

The trail leads through a forest of larch, ponderosa pine, western white pine, mountain hemlock, and subalpine fir. Negotiate a couple of big switchbacks, and the grade eases. As you near the basin the surrounding boggy areas may reveal whether you'll have company at the lake. Your pooch may already have picked up that this is moose country.

If the moose aren't there, chances are good that you and your dog will have the lake to yourselves. Pick a flat rock to sit on and enjoy watching the small cascade at the far end of the lake. There is another lake beyond, but it's a tough bushwhack into prime grizzly country. Anyway, with your sunbathing rock providing front row seats to serene Bramlet Lake, is there any reason to push farther?

71. Upper Geiger Lake– Lost Buck Pass

Location: Cabinet Mountains
Round Trip to Upper Geiger Lake: 7.5 miles
Hiking Time: 5 hours
High Point: 5400 feet
Elevation Gain: 1600 feet
Maps: USFS Cabinet Mountains Wilderness, or USGS Howard Lake
Best Hiking Time: late June to October
Contact: Kootenai National Forest, Libby Ranger District,
    (406) 293-8861, (406) 827-3534

Driving Directions: From Libby, Montana, head east on US Highway 2 for 24 miles. Immediately before milepost 57 and the bridge across Fisher River, turn right onto Forest Road 231 (West Fisher Creek Road). Follow this road for 5.5 miles and turn left on FR 2332. Proceed on this road for 0.75 mile, passing Lake Creek Campground. In 2 miles you'll come to the Fourth of July Trailhead, with its horse ramp on your left.

The Geiger Lakes are definitely two of the more discovered spots in the Cabinet Mountains Wilderness. Easy access, good fishing, good camping, and nice scenery—it all adds up to lots of hikers. But here's a little secret for you and your pup, a chance for the two of you to enjoy this area without encountering a lot of fellow trail users. The majority of hikers come to this area via Geiger Lakes Trail 656. Very few take to the Fourth of July Creek Trail 115.

"Why?" you may ask. Most hikers are content with going to the lower lake only. Trail 115 skips it and heads directly to the upper lake. The trade-off? You get to hike through a beautiful forest and along a rushing stream most of the way with very little chance of bumping into anyone. Besides, the lower lake is nice but not spectacular. It's the upper lake and the country beyond it that is truly breathtaking. Plus you'll skip the steep climb

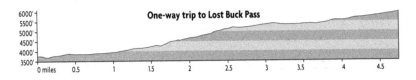

on the Geiger Lakes Trail and stay well away from the mosquito-infested bogs that ring the lower lake.

Are you sold now on the Fourth of July Creek Trail? Good! The trail begins by immediately crossing Bramlet Creek on a sturdy bridge. It's now a gradual climb through a forest of larch, cedar, and lodgepole pine. Clumps of bear grass, more than 6 feet high in places, line the trail. You may lose your dog in it! In 1.25 miles you'll come to Fourth of July Creek. Pass the ruins of an old cabin and in 2 miles cross the creek, a great spot to take a break before the climb stiffens a little.

In 3 miles you'll cross the wilderness boundary and not far beyond come to the junction with Trail 656. Follow this trail right and in 0.5 mile you'll come to the short Spur Trail 48, which leads to Upper Geiger Lake (5360 ft.). It's a pretty spot, flanked by mountain hemlocks, subalpine meadows, and rugged ridges. Carney Peak (7173 ft.) and Ferrell's Wall add rugged touches along the western shore. Camping is good once the snow melts, usually by mid-July.

If you and your pal want to see more of the surrounding country, consider hiking Trail 656 another 1.25 miles to Lost Buck Pass (6000 ft.). Sprawling meadows and dazzling views await, especially over Upper Geiger Lake and the wild Swamp Creek Basin to the west. Wanless Lake, one of the more remote and wild of the Cabinet Lakes, can be viewed by walking just a few minutes south along the Cabinet Divide Trail 360. It

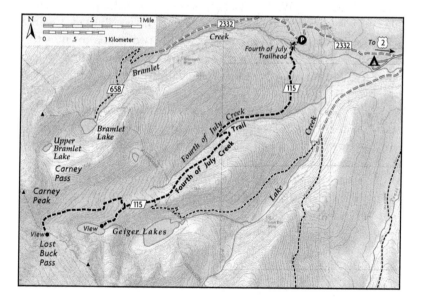

Enjoying view from Lost Buck Pass (Photo by Craig Romano)

is a breathtaking vista. If you care to continue, Trail 360 makes a skyline journey southward for over 10 miles. Sure-footed dogs should be comfortable along the way, but patches of scree may be difficult for some pooches. Water is scarce after the snow melts. Of course, you can always head back to Upper Geiger and let your buddy play in the sparkling waters.

72. Cabin Lake

Location: Cabinet Mountains
Round Trip: 5 miles
Hiking Time: 3 hours
High Point: 5900 feet
Elevation Gain: 1150 feet
Loop Trip through Four Lakes Basin: 8 miles
Hiking Time: 5 hours
High Point: 6500 feet
Elevation Gain: 2150 feet
Maps: USGS Mount Headley, Priscilla Peak
Best Hiking Time: June through October
Contact: Lolo National Forest, Plains/Thompson Falls Ranger District, (406) 826-3821

Driving Directions: From Thompson Falls, Montana, drive east on State Route 200 for 5 miles. At milepost 56 turn left (north) onto the paved

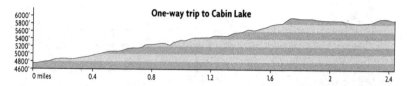

Thompson River Road, signed "County Road 556." This road becomes Forest Road 56. The pavement ends after 4 miles at a national forest campground. After 6.5 miles from SR 200 you'll come to an intersection. Bear left on FR 603, signed "Four Lakes Trailhead 8 miles." Follow this rocky road 7.75 miles to its end at the trailhead.

The proposed Cube Iron-Silcox Wilderness area of the southern Cabinet Mountains offers miles of great backcountry romps into a lightly traveled region. Lofty summits, alpine meadows and lakes, and a good trail system characterize this roadless area just north of Thompson Falls. Hikers and their dogs will find a number of trails and destinations to their liking. Cabin Lake stands out as one of the supreme choices in this de facto wilderness.

The hike to Cabin Lake, one of the largest bodies of water within the Cube Iron-Silcox, is pretty straightforward. From the trailhead take Trail 459 right across a sturdy bridge. On an old road-turned-trail begin

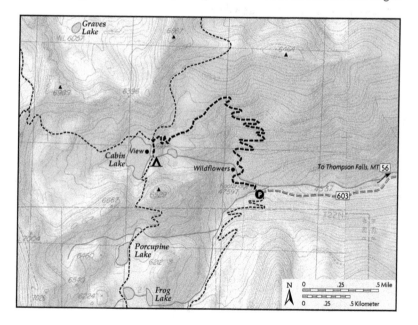

Tank in camp along the shore of Cabin Lake

climbing through an old cut. In 10 minutes you'll come to the creek that drains Cabin Lake. This is the last time that you will see any water until you arrive at the lake in 2.25 miles. After some steady climbing through mature timber, Trail 459 comes to an end at Trail 450, the Thompson-Headley Trail. This excellent high-country trail traverses 15 miles across the proposed wilderness area, from Mount Headley in the north to Weber Gulch in the south, just outside of Thompson Falls.

From this junction turn left (south) and hike 5 minutes, passing another trail junction (Winneimuck Trail 506) to Cabin Lake. The two of you will have no problem whiling away the time at this pretty mountain lake. Good spots for sitting and swimming exist near some well-used campsites close to the outlet creek. Lots of jumping fish will pique your dog's interest.

For more secluded spots along the lake continue hiking south on Trail 459. The trail hugs Cabin's shore for a short way before climbing steeply up the ridge that separates Cabin from the Four Lakes basin. By continuing to the Four Lakes basin and hiking back to the trailhead utilizing Trail 460, the two of you can complete a nice 8-mile loop. The trail through the basin is in good shape, but the hike out follows a trail that was once a logging road. If your dog can handle rocky walking then by all means hike the loop.

The four lakes that sit in the basin (there are actually more, but they're small and unnamed)—Porcupine, Frog, Grass, and Knowles—are shallower than Cabin and are ringed by dense forest. They tend to harbor a few mosquitoes, too. Still, they make for a pretty hike and there is always the chance of spotting a moose.

Trail 460 leaves Trail 459 about 2.5 miles from Cabin Lake. The junction is easy to miss. If you begin climbing towards Squaw Pass, you've missed it. The hike out on Trail 460 follows Four Lakes Creek 3 miles back to the trailhead.

Note: A nice side trip can be made by hiking 0.25 mile to Squaw Pass, then following a 0.5-mile spur trail to the old lookout site on 7179-foot Cube Iron Mountain. The views are incredible, from the Bitterroot Divide to the Cabinet Wilderness Peaks. Dogs shouldn't have any trouble on this trail, but it is in open meadows and can be hot during the summer.

73. Deer Lake

Location: Cabinet Mountains
Round Trip: 7 miles
Hiking Time: 4–5 hours
High Point: 5928 feet
Elevation Gain: 2600 feet
Maps: USGS Mount Headley, Priscilla Peak
Best Hiking Time: June through October
Contact: Lolo National Forest, Plains/Thompson Falls Ranger District, (406) 826-3821

Driving Directions: From Thompson Falls, Montana, drive east on State Route 200 for 5 miles. At milepost 56 turn left onto the paved Thompson River Road, signed "County Road 556." This road becomes Forest Road

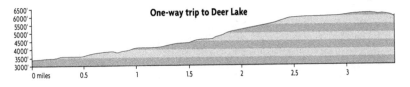

56. The pavement ends after 4 miles at a national forest campground. After 6.5 miles from SR 200 you'll come to an intersection. Bear left on FR 603, signed "Four Lake Trailhead 8 miles." Follow this road for just under 2 miles to a junction. Turn left onto FR 7657 (signed "Honeymoon Creek Trailhead") and proceed on this rough road 1.5 miles to the trailhead. The trail begins at a bend where the road crosses Honeymoon Creek. Park on the shoulder just past the trailhead.

Are you looking for a quiet alternative to Cabin Lake? An alpine lake that you and your dog can enjoy all by yourselves? A place where you might actually be able to catch a fish, without worrying that your dog may scare them all away? Deer Lake might be what you have in mind. However, this lake is not attained without expending an incredible amount of energy. Although it's only a 3.5-mile hike, there are 2600 feet of elevation gain and most of them are between mile one and two, the dreaded "middle mile." So, if you and your buddy are in top-dog shape, go for it. There's a great little lake waiting, one that only a handful of rugged hikers and hounds have ever seen.

Trail 469 begins by following Honeymoon Creek through a cool, shaded forest. Though a little brushy in the beginning, the trail soon improves. After 0.5 mile you'll cross the creek. Alternating between short, steep sections and saner segments, the entire climb is shady, passing first

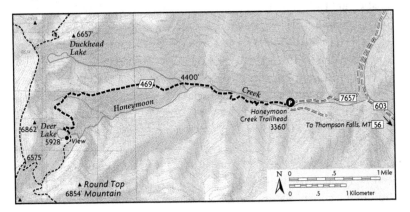

Deer Lake (Photo by Craig Romano)

under a thick canopy of regenerating forest, then through old-growth cedars, and finally through a healthy stand of pine and larch.

After crossing a damp gulch the trail comes pretty close to Honeymoon Creek for one last time. Fill water bottles here—it's a dry ascent to Deer Lake. About one-third of the way there the trail shows you what the word "steep" really means.

At about 2.5 miles, relief is finally granted. Now the trail works its way into a hidden basin and rounds a steep slope to the basin that houses Deer Lake. The trees thin, providing a good vista of the east. Prominent peaks—Big Hole, Priscilla, and Baldy—dominate the view. You can also see where you came from—what an insane climb!

Rounding the ridge through a forest of white bark and lodgepole pine, the trail drops in one switchback (the only one on this hike) to the semi-open bowl containing dear old Deer Lake. Take your pack off, swig some water, and enjoy! You both have earned it. There are some good campsites just above the outlet and across the lake on an overlooking bluff. The lake and its surroundings are pretty, but it's the solitude that really makes this hike.

If you're not content with the climbing thus far, the tiny Goat Lakes can be reached by hiking 1 mile more up the trail. What's a few more hundred feet of elevation gain?

TEN LAKES SCENIC AREA

74. Bluebird Lake–Highline

Location: Ten Lakes Scenic Area
Round Trip to Bluebird Lake: 5 miles
Hiking Time: 3 hours
High Point: 6800 feet
Elevation Gain: 850 feet
Map: USGS Ksanka Peak
Best Hiking Time: July to late September
Contact: Kootenai National Forest, Fortine District, Murphy Lake
   Ranger Station, (406) 882-4451

Driving Directions: From Eureka, Montana, head south on US Highway 93 for 9 miles. Turn left onto Forest Road 114 (Graves Creek), signed "Therriault Lakes/Ten Lakes Scenic Area 28 miles." From Whitefish, Montana, head north on US 93 for 42 miles, turning right onto FR 114. Follow FR 114 (pavement ends after 10 miles) for 14 miles where it merges with FR 319. Continue straight on FR 319 (following signs for Therriault

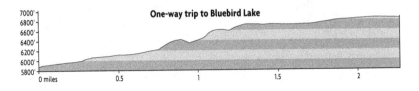

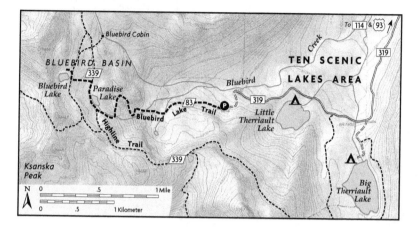

Lakes) for 15.75 miles, passing the campgrounds on Big and Little Therriault Lakes, to the road's end and the trailhead for Bluebird Trail 83.

If the Ten Lakes Scenic Area were any more accessible it would certainly be overrun by visitors. Fortunately they're tucked in a quiet corner of Montana, far away from any major communities. It's a trek getting here, so why not spend the weekend? Consider car camping at Big or Little Therriault Lakes—then it's just a roll out of your sleeping bag to all of this splendid backcountry.

Bluebird Lake is a great place to begin. With a trailhead elevation over 5800 feet, hoofing to the 6700-foot-high lake could hardly be easier. Snow remains in the basin well into July, so finding water is never a problem. The only concern that you and your four-legged companion should have is that this is some of the best grizzly habitat within the Inland Northwest. Chances are you'll never see one of these monarchs of the mountains, but keep your friend nearby and stay alert. There are usually fresh tracks along the way.

Bluebird Lake Trail 83 begins in a clear-cut but soon enters a cool old-growth forest. Keep your eyes (or in your dog's case, ears) peeled for spruce grouse. In 0.5 mile you'll come to the first of many stream crossings, some bridged, some not. None are particularly challenging.

After a little climbing, in 1.75 miles the trail delivers you to a tranquil subalpine forest ringing serene little Paradise Lake (6720 ft.). You'll be hard-pressed to argue the appropriateness of the name. Linger for a while, soak your feet in the shallow water. But before the two of you get too comfortable, remember that Bluebird Lake is even more inviting.

Doug Romano at Bluebird Lake (Photo by Craig Romano)

Five minutes beyond Paradise Lake is a four-way junction. Turn right on Highline Trail 339 and walk another 5 minutes to a second junction. Take the spur trail left to Bluebird Lake. It's another 5 minutes of hiking through some of the prettiest country this side of Glacier National Park. Matter of fact, you can see the towering peaks of Glacier from the outlet of the lake. Bluebird Lake itself (6800 ft.) is quite a sight, surrounded by meadows and subalpine forest on one side and steep, rocky ridges on the other.

You and your intrepid pup can easily while away the rest of the day at Bluebird Lake, but if you're intent on seeing more of the Ten Lakes Scenic Area, consider a jaunt on the Highline. Either direction is fine. Left (north) goes to open Bluebird Basin and Green Mountain, right (south) goes all the way to Mount Wam, about 8 miles away. By utilizing the Little Therriault Loop Tie-in Trail 85, it's a 3.5-mile hike back to Little Therriault Lake Campground. Walk the road 0.5 mile back to the trailhead for a nice 6.5-mile loop.

75. Stahl Peak Lookout

Location: Ten Lakes Scenic Area
Round Trip: 7 miles
Hiking Time: 4 hours
High Point: 7435 feet
Elevation Gain: 1700 feet
Map: USGS Stahl Peak
Best Hiking Time: July to late September
Contact: Kootenai National Forest, Fortine Ranger Station, (406) 882-4451

Driving Directions: From Eureka, Montana, head south on US Highway 93 for 9 miles. Turn left onto Forest Road 114 (Graves Creek), signed "Therriault Lakes/Ten Lakes Scenic Area 28 miles." From Whitefish, Montana, head north on US 93 for 42 miles, turning right onto FR 114. Follow FR 114 (pavement ends after 10 miles) for 14 miles where it

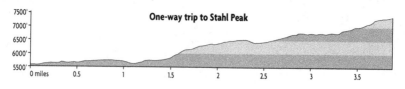

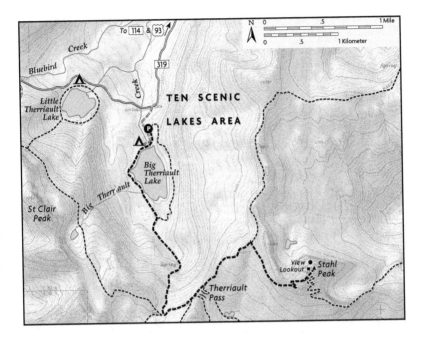

merges with FR 319. Continue straight on FR 319 (following signs for Therriault Lakes) 14 miles to Big Therriault Lake. The trail begins from the campground.

The Ten Lakes Scenic Area is one of the jewels of the Kootenai National Forest. Straddling the Canadian border about halfway between Glacier National Park and the Purcell Mountains of the Yaak River Country, this 7000-acre parcel along with 33,000 acres of surrounding high country has been proposed for inclusion in the federal wilderness system. It should be. With over a dozen alpine lakes and eight peaks over 7000 feet, this high-country region remains relatively pristine in a national forest that has been intensively logged. This is prime grizzly habitat, with unbroken old-growth forests and sprawling alpine meadows.

With almost 90 miles of trail, there's plenty of beautiful backcountry for you and your poochie to explore. Consider base camping at Big or Little Therriault Lake to allow the two of you maximum time in this remote corner of Big Sky Country. The hike to Stahl Lookout affords you an eagle's-eye view of this primeval paradise. Best of all, this hike begins right from Big Therriault Lake and includes a walk along the shores of this lovely body of water.

Stahl Peak Lookout (Photo by Craig Romano)

From the campground, Trail 190 departs for the lake through a cool and damp forest. Your pal may be intent on a swim in the inviting lake, but that can wait for the return. The area surrounding Big Therriault is quite boggy and buggy by midsummer. Further incentive to head for the high country. Keep your eyes out for moose and be sure that your furry friend is near your side. Moose and grizzly frequent these woods.

In 0.75 mile, just beyond the bridge crossing of Big Therriault Creek, you'll come to the junction with the Big Therriault Loop Trail 86. Consider returning this way to the campground on your journey back from Stahl.

Beyond the lake the trail traverses a wildlife-rich area of expansive marshes, open forest, and rushing streams. In 1.25 miles you'll reach a creek crossing and, depending on the time of the year, quite possibly your last source of water. Pack plenty for the two of you.

The grade steepens and after a series of switchbacks you'll reach a junction with the Highline Trail 339 at 2 miles (6400 ft.). Head left on the Highline (right goes to Bluebird Lake, Hike 74). After about 30 minutes of steady climbing you'll come to the junction with Stahl Peak Trail 81 at about 2.5 miles (6750 ft.). Prepare yourself for an "elevated" adventure. In 1 mile, after two short and one long switchback, you'll emerge on the summit (7435 ft.). Be sure to take the summit spur-trail, because Trail 81 continues down the south side of the mountain.

The summit of Stahl is broad, but keep Fido nearby because there's one heck of a drop on the north side. Soak up the warming sun and the expansive views. High peaks from Glacier National Park and the Cabinet Wilderness pierce the horizon. The entire green swath of the Ten Lakes Scenic Area sprawls below you. To the northeast, 7203-foot Mount Wam, with its fire lookout, appears as a mirror image of Stahl.

And speaking of the Stahl Lookout, feel free to spend the night in it. There's no charge, and it's open on a first-come basis. Your buddy is welcome to spend the night inside with you. Be sure to pack a blanket for him.

APPENDIX A: RECOMMENDED READING

Acker, Randy. *Field Guide: Dog First Aid Emergency Care for the Hunting, Working, and Outdoor Dog.* Gallatin Gateway, Mont.: Wilderness Adventures Press, 1994.

Anderson, Kristi and Arleen Tavernier. *Wilderness Basics.* Seattle, Wash.: Mountaineers Books, 2004.

Fogle, Bruce and Amanda Williams. *First Aid for Dogs: What to Do When Emergencies Happen.* New York, N.Y.: Penguin, 1997.

LaBelle, Charlene G. *Guide to Backpacking with Your Dog.* Loveland, Colo.: Alpine Publications, 1992.

Mullally, Linda. *Hiking with Dogs: Becoming a Wilderness-Wise Dog Owner.* Missoula, Mont.: Falcon Guides, 1999.

Romano, Craig. "Running with Dogs." *Northwest Runner Magazine,* June 2004, pp. 44–46.

Smith, Cheryl S. *On the Trail with Your Canine Companion: Getting the Most out of Hiking and Camping with your Dog.* New York, N.Y.: Howell Book/ Macmillan, 1996.

Doggie Publications

DogFancy magazine is a monthly covering all aspects of canine living.
www.dogfancy.com

For the pooch on the go; check out *Fido Friendly, The Travel Magazine for Dogs.*
www.fidofriendly.com

Computer-savvy mutts may want to consult *Good Dog!,* an online publication.
www.gooddogmagazine.com

APPENDIX B: HIKES THAT ORIGINATE FROM DEVELOPED CAMPGROUNDS

1. Hike 1 Tiffany Mountain and Lake
2. Hike 5 Swan Lake and Butte
3. Hike 8 Collier Lakes
4. Hike 10 Granby River
5. Hike 11 Deer Point-Christina Lake
6. Hike 14 Champion Lakes
7. Hike 18 Lockhart Creek
8. Hike 22 Wapaloosie Mountain
9. Hike 26 Emerald Lake
10. Hike 28 South Fork Silver Creek
11. Hike 29 Sullivan Lake
12. Hike 30 Noisy Creek-Hall Mountain
13. Hike 33 Salmo Loop-Little Snowy Top
14. Hike 38 Oregon Butte Grand Loop
15. Hike 39 Puffer Butte
16. Hike 40 Day Mountain Loop-Mount Spokane State Park
17. Hike 42 Liberty Lake Loop
18. Hike 44 Kamiak Butte
19. Hike 45 Indian Cliff
20. Hike 46 Mary Minerva McCroskey Country
21. Hike 47 Priest Lake-Lakeshore Trail
22. Hike 56 Upper St. Joe River
23. Hike 57 Mallard Lake and Peak
24. Hike 63 Diamond and Cliff Lakes
25. Hike 74 Bluebird Lake-Highline
26. Hike 75 Stahl Peak Lookout

Sailor along the Snow Lake Trail

APPENDIX C: DOGGIE GEAR AND RESOURCES

Doggie backpacks can be found at Granite Gear.
www.granitegear.com

Planetdog is an excellent source for all types of gear for your hiking hound.
www.planetdog.com

Ruffwear is another fine company offering a myriad of products for your trekking terrier.
www.ruffwear.com

1-800-PetMeds will supply your mutt with all of his medications.
www.1800petmeds.com

If you are looking for a new companion, consider *www.petfinder.com.* This is how Mittens found Alan!

Other places to find Inland Northwest dogs include:

Spokane County Animal Shelter
2521 N. Flora Road
Spokane Valley, WA 99216-1806
Phone: (509) 477-2532

Panhandle Animal Shelter
1604 Great Northern Road
Sandpoint, ID 83864
Phone: (208) 265-7297

Coeur d'Alene Animal Shelter
1902 Fourth Street
Coeur d'Alene, ID 83814
Phone: (208) 665-7379

Late winter waterfall tumbles toward Dusty Lake.

Whitman County Humane Society
635 NW Guy
Pullman, WA 99163
(509) 332-2246
www.whitmanpets.org

INDEX

ABOUT THE AUTHORS

(Photo by Heather Scott)

Craig Romano

Hiking is a way of life for Craig. From Quebec to Argentina, Slovenia to South Korea, he enjoys "discovering" new places. The Inland Northwest is one of his favorite haunts. A marathon runner, kayaker, and skier, he has also cycled across North America three times. He holds a BA in history and a graduate degree in education. His work as a freelance writer and photographer has appeared in several magazines including *Backpacker, Canoe and Kayak, Northwest Travel, Northwest Outdoors, AMC Outdoors,* and *Northwest Runner.* He also writes recreational content for *Greentrails.com, MountainZone.com,* and Canada's *theweathernetwork.com.* He contributed to *Best Wildflower Hikes in Washington* (Mountaineers Books). When not writing about hiking, Craig shares his enthusiasm for the mountains with others. He works part time in Europe as a guide for Walking Softly Adventures.

Alan L. Bauer

Alan L. Bauer is a professional freelance photographer specializing in the natural history of the Pacific Northwest and coverage of local history. He is a lifelong resident of the Pacific Northwest, having grown up on a large farm in Oregon's Willamette Valley and having called Washington State his home for the past 17 years.

His work has been published in *Backpacker, Northwest Runner, SportsEtc, Northwest Outdoors, Redmond Reporter, The Tacoma News Tribune, The Bellingham Herald, Oregon Coast,* and *Northwest Travel* as well as the Getaways weekly outdoor recreation magazine insert for the *Seattle Post-Intelligencer.* He has been a long-time contributor to *Signpost* for Northwest Trails / Washington Trails, the monthly magazine published by The Washington Trails Association. His photographs were featured throughout the NW Hiking section of the Northwest Cable News (NWCN) weekly television program and website, and in recreation reports for the The Weather Network of Canada. Alan writes a monthly column, "Natural Neighbors," for his local community newsletter (*Fall City Neighbors*) where he shares his knowledge of regional natural history.

His photographs have recently been published in the music CD layout design for Scott D. Davis' newest recordings *Tahoma* and *Winter Journey.*

Alan's most recent book, *Best Desert Hikes: Washington* was published in October 2004. His first project with The Mountaineers Books, *Best Loop Hikes: Washington* was published in spring 2003. You can contact Alan at *http:// www.alanbauer.com.*

Ghiry on the shores of Christina Lake at Deer Point

THE MOUNTAINEERS, founded in 1906, is a nonprofit outdoor activity and conservation club, whose mission is "to explore, study, preserve, and enjoy the natural beauty of the outdoors. . . . " Based in Seattle, Washington, the club is now one of the largest such organizations in the United States, with seven branches throughout Washington State.

The Mountaineers sponsors both classes and year-round outdoor activities in the Pacific Northwest, which include hiking, mountain climbing, ski-touring, snowshoeing, bicycling, camping, kayaking, nature study, sailing, and adventure travel. The club's conservation division supports environmental causes through educational activities, sponsoring legislation, and presenting informational programs.

All club activities are led by skilled, experienced instructors, who are dedicated to promoting safe and responsible enjoyment and preservation of the outdoors.

If you would like to participate in these organized outdoor activities or the club's programs, consider a membership in The Mountaineers. For information and an application, write or call The Mountaineers, Program Center, 7700 Sand Point Way NE, Seattle, WA 98115; (206) 521-6001. You can also visit their website at www.mountaineers.org or contact The Mountaineers via email at info@mountaineers.org.

The Mountaineers Books, an active, nonprofit publishing program of the club, produces guidebooks, instructional texts, historical works, natural history guides, and works on environmental conservation. All books produced by The Mountaineers Books fulfill the club's mission.

Send or call for our catalog of more than 500 outdoor titles

 The Mountaineers Books
1001 SW Klickitat Way, Suite 201
Seattle, WA 98134
(800) 553-4453
mbooks@mountaineersbooks.org
www.mountaineersbooks.org

 The Mountaineers Books is proud to be a corporate sponsor of Leave No Trace, whose mission is to promote and inspire responsible outdoor recreation through education, research, and partnerships. The Leave No Trace program is focused specifically on human-powered (nonmotorized) recreation.

Leave No Trace strives to educate visitors about the nature of their recreational impacts, as well as offer techniques to prevent and minimize such impacts. Leave No Trace is best understood as an educational and ethical program, not as a set of rules and regulations.

For more information, visit *www.lnt.org,* or call 800-332-4100.

OTHER TITLES YOU MIGHT ENJOY
FROM THE MOUNTAINEERS BOOKS

**Best Hikes with Dogs
Western Washington, 2nd Edition**
Dan Nelson
From Puget Sound and the Olympics, to
the Cascades—85 trails for dogs to roam

**Best Hikes with Dogs Oregon,
2nd Edition**
Ellen Morris Bishop
76 hikes around the state for all
skill levels of dog and owners

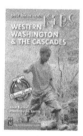

**Best Hikes with Kids
Western Washington & the Cascades**
Joan Burton
Easy day hikes for the whole family
covering Mount Rainier, the San Juan
Islands, Stevens Pass and the
Olympic Peninsula.

100 Classic Hikes in Washington
Ira Spring & Harvey Manning
A full-color guide to Washington's
finest trails, written with a conservation
ethic, and featuring some of
the best hikes in the state.